Jesus' Awkward Questions

Philip Yeung

Published by Yeung E Publishing, 2021.

Jesus' Awkward Questions

Dr. Philip Yeung

Unless otherwise stated, all Scripture quotations are taken from the Holy Bible, New International Version®, NIV®. Copyright ©1973, 1978, 1984, 2011 by Biblica, Inc.® Used by permission. All rights reserved worldwide.

Cover design by Joanie Yeung

ISBN: 9798201322373 (paperback)
9798201353797 (e-book)

Table of Contents

Glory to our Creator

Foreword

What happens when you ask a professional Bible scholar to preach a sermon? Sometimes it can be a disaster. It is one thing to stand before a class to explain some difficult concept in Hebrew or Greek; it is quite another to stand before a congregation to expound a biblical text with simplicity and clarity. In the life of Philip Yeung we have someone who was able to do both with professional competence and pastoral warmth.

I first knew Philip as a student in one of my Hebrew classes in 1978-79 at Regent College in Vancouver. Philip was the best student in the class, always exact in his recall of difficult forms and clear in his answer to challenging questions. I wondered what the future was going to be for this brilliant student, already a trained and accredited medical doctor. Surely it would be a flourishing academic career in some prestigious institution. Indeed, Philip did become an excellent scholar in a highly regarded theological college, but throughout his life Philip never lost his passion for helping people of all backgrounds, students and laity alike, to understand the scriptures in all their profundity as well as in their practical application to life.

This collection of sermons by Philip preached at Emmanuel Chinese Church in Hong Kong puts the reader/listener in the hands of a first rate scholar and at the same time a practically minded preacher. We can trust his clarification of Greek words even as our minds are illuminated and our hearts are warmed by his intimate knowledge of the complexities of modern life, whether in Hong Kong or elsewhere. Bringing both together is never an easy task. Philip, by the grace of God, was gifted to do both.

Sven Soderlund
Professor Emeritus of Biblical Studies
Regent College, Vancouver

Preface

Ever since I was very young, I have known that my father, the late Pastor and Doctor Philip Yeung, absolutely loved the Bible. For him, the Bible was a vast treasure trove which he spent much of his life digging into to uncover new treasures each time. Contrary to many people's expectations, he never told me and my sister to read the Bible. But simply by watching the way he studied it, we learned as children that the Bible is a very precious and exciting book.

My father had a habit of annotating his bibles. The empty spaces on countless pages were filled with very tiny scribbled notes in English, Chinese, Greek, and Hebrew that are hardly legible or comprehensible to other people. He also used a unique system of symbols that he created for himself to represent certain words, and claimed that only he could decipher them.

His decision to give up his medical profession to teach in a Bible seminary shocked many people at the time in the materialistic society of Hong Kong. But every time he shared the story, he was filled with joy and conviction, seeing it as the best decision he could have ever made in his whole life, like the man who sold everything in exchange for a pearl (Matthew 13:45–46).

My father joined the China Graduate School of Theology (CGST) in Hong Kong in 1980, and worked there for 40 years in various roles until he was taken home to be with the Lord. The School is renowned for its pastoral, biblical and intellectual training of a whole generation of pastors and

Christian workers in both Hong Kong and abroad, and my father devoted his life to this mission. To his friends and students, he was best known as "Yeung E", 'E' being the homonym for the word 'doctor' in Chinese. Proficient in Biblical Greek and Hebrew, he was able to teach both languages at graduate level. His teaching focused on applying the Bible to everyday life, opening new perspectives on creation, suffering, the Christian identity, Sabbath rest, vocational calling, and Christianity in the marketplace. For him, salvation is not just about going to heaven sometime in the future; he firmly believed that God's will for us is as clear and as down-to-earth as it can be here and now.

My father's passion for studying the original Hebrew texts of Genesis Chapters 1–3 led to his development of what he called the Creation Theology—a system of theology for seeing God's sovereign will in the physical, functional, and moral orders within the created world, and for understanding how the Creator relates to us in our lives. This Creation Theology opens doors to Biblical teachings that tend to be neglected in much contemporary preaching, especially regarding wisdom literature in the Bible. He saw that the book of Job is as important as the Gospel of John; Genesis is as relevant as Galatians; and Ecclesiastes is as pertinent as Ephesians. He believed that this aspect of Bible teaching is sadly missing from many churches, and he wanted to demonstrate how Creation Theology can helpfully complement our understanding of what Jesus accomplished on the cross.

In September 2020, my father was called home to be with the Lord after a short but fierce battle with pancreatic cancer. One of the legacies he has left is a collection of his sermons and teachings. My family and I plan to translate many of his talks from Chinese to English, so that non-Chinese-speaking believers and seekers, including some of my dad's friends and relatives, will be able to benefit from his sermons too.

Jesus' Awkward Questions is the first such project. It is a collection of twelve sermons he preached at Emmanuel Chinese Church, Hong Kong, over a span of eleven years (with several of the chapters taken from his sermon series, "Jesus Asks You"). Each chapter of the book focuses on a story in which Jesus asked a seemingly strange question, and reflects on what Jesus was revealing about himself, the human condition, and how Jesus relates to us today. Applying his knowledge of biblical Greek, my father dissected the texts by looking at the Gospel authors' original word choices and expressions in the historical and cultural contexts of the Ancient Near East.

Translating sermons from the spoken form into written form is not a straightforward process. This book aims to retain all the core messages of the sermons, but certain details that are specific to the internal or local contexts of Emmanuel Chinese Church in Hong Kong have been edited.

This book can be used for personal reflection and devotion, or as material for discipleship group discussions. At the end of the book is a list of questions that can be used as a discussion guide. Our sincere hope is that this book will be helpful both to Christians who have walked with the Lord for some time as well as seekers of the Christian faith who are getting to know Jesus. Perhaps as you reflect on the questions Jesus asked two thousands ago, you will find God asking you questions you have never thought of.

Joanie Yeung

1.

Why are you searching for me?

(Luke 2:39-52)

39 When Joseph and Mary had done everything required by the Law of the Lord, they returned to Galilee to their own town of Nazareth. **40** And the child grew and became strong; he was filled with wisdom, and the grace of God was on him.

41 Every year Jesus' parents went to Jerusalem for the Festival of the Passover. **42** When he was twelve years old, they went up to the festival, according to the custom. **43** After the festival was over, while his parents were returning home, the boy Jesus stayed behind in Jerusalem, but they were unaware of it. **44** Thinking he was in their company, they traveled on for a day. Then they began looking for him among their relatives and friends. **45** When they did not find him, they went back to Jerusalem to look for him. **46** After three days they found him in the temple courts, sitting among the teachers, listening to them and asking them questions. **47** Everyone who heard him was amazed at his understanding and his answers. **48** When his parents saw him, they were astonished. His mother said to him, "Son, why have you treated us like this? Your father and I have been anxiously searching for you." **49** "Why were you searching for me?" he asked. "Didn't you know I had to be in my Father's house?" **50** But they did not understand what he was saying to them. **51** Then he went down to Nazareth with them and was obedient to them. But his mother treasured all these things in her heart. **52** And Jesus grew in wisdom and stature, and in favour with God and man.

"Why are you searching for me?"

This is not only Jesus' first question recorded in the Gospels, but also his earliest direct conversation quoted in the Bible. Strangely enough, it was a question he asked his mother, who was searching for him when he was lost!

Whenever we want to learn about a historical figure or celebrity, we read the person's autobiography or biography. Books in this genre almost always devote a substantial portion of the writing to depicting snapshots of the person's childhood. Everyone's childhood has unique stories to tell and interesting encounters that have shaped the person's identity and future. So what happens when four authors from the first century with a professed interest in the life of Jesus each tried to write a book on Jesus? We might expect to read at least a few miraculous signs and extraordinary details from Jesus' childhood that set him apart from all other children.

Yet surprisingly, the Bible hardly gives us any such details. We know almost nothing about the 30 years of Jesus' life between his birth and his baptism that took place just before he began his ministry as an adult. So what happened to Jesus during all those formative years of his life?

The one and only account we have regarding Jesus' childhood in all four Gospels can be found at the end of Luke chapter 2. Luke set out to write a book to prove Jesus is the Son of God, the Messiah the world had been waiting for. As a medical doctor, he would have had a keen interest in the developmental stages of the child Jesus. Yet even for Luke, there was only one story to tell. As far as the doctor was concerned, apart from the fact that Jesus was born of a virgin, Jesus was like any other human child. Jesus came to this world as a newborn baby and grew up as a normal child.

When did Jesus come to terms with his calling to die on the cross? How did he process his identity as the Son of God? We do not know, because the Bible never tells us. Luke summarized Jesus' growth and development in one very simple line in verse 40:

> **40** And the child grew and became strong; he was filled with wisdom, and the grace of God was upon him.

The words 'grew' and 'became' both indicate it was a prolonged, gradual process. These two verbs can be applied to the developmental growth of any human being. Jesus was fully human not only in appearance, but also in his experience of going through each stage of life. These verbs also imply there was a time when Jesus was not yet fully grown or full of strength. There was a time when Jesus was still 'not there yet' and needed time to grow. God did not send His Son to the world as an almighty, omniscient, fully-grown man with a halo, or a prodigy child reciting Scriptures, but as a needy baby who needed time to grow slowly in every way. Jesus started from zero just like you and me. So Jesus' childhood was made up of small, normal learning stages.

Are we surprised? What does this mean to us? Couldn't God skip all the hassle and save lots of time by simply sending Jesus as a fully-developed superman ready to teach, heal the sick, and die on the cross straight away? Imagine how much trouble this would have saved Mary and Joseph all those years!

Yet that was not God's will or plan. The Word became flesh and dwelled among us as 100% human. This involved going through 100% of the growing stages and processes of human life. In God's creation, there are no shortcuts or crash courses. Have you noticed all examples of growth in the Bible, both physical and spiritual, are slow and gradual? The one and only exceptional case we can find is the vine that appeared at the end of Jonah's story. God made a vine grow up quickly to give shade to the angry Jonah, but it quickly withered and died the next day when a worm chewed it (Jonah 4:6-7). The only example of instant growth in the Bible did not have a good ending at all. Similarly, in our body, the only type of fast-growing development is usually what we call 'cancer'. In God's design, everything good takes its own time. God is never in a hurry.

However, we like it the other way round. We expect our efforts to yield instant results. We want to become a godly, mature Christian right now. We want to bear lots of fruit immediately. We want to have patience straight away. We want our sins and bad habits to be totally gone by tomorrow.

Indeed, God's healing and transformation can also happen quickly and bring miraculous change in ways beyond our imagination. But growth is not to be confused with healing. Growth is a process, and the process is a part of God's plan. Jesus went through this process at the same pace that we do. Did Jesus fall when he was learning to walk? Did he cry like a normal child? Did he learn Hebrew and Greek from scratch by painstakingly memorizing each letter of the alphabet like my seminary students have to? Did he learn Scriptures gradually like we all do as well? The Bible does not say directly, but I believe so, though it might be hard for us to imagine our Lord and Saviour going through all these stages.

Now let's go back to the story.

Jesus was 12 years old; he was taken by his parents to the temple in Jerusalem as part of the Jewish customs during the Feast. From the context of the story, we can speculate that the children and their parents had separate activities during the events. There was probably a large children's programme where Jesus and other children learned about the Scriptures. At the time, Scriptures were hand-copied and stored mainly in temples and synagogues in big cities. So it would have been a fascinating experience for a child from Nazareth to be attending a big religious 'conference' in Jerusalem. Jesus probably became so preoccupied that he did not reunite with his parents afterwards when they were expecting him. This would be any parent's worst nightmare. Imagine losing your child for three days at a huge religious festival. What could be going through your mind?

Now, imagine two parents, at the point of exploding with anxiety, finally finding their lost child. What would they say to one another? In verses 48-49,

> **48** When his parents saw him, they were astonished. His mother said to him, "Son, why have you treated us like this? Your father and I have been anxiously searching for you."

> **49** "Why were you searching for me?" he asked. "Didn't you know I had to be in my Father's house?"

In verse 49, the last word 'house' was not in the original text. Jesus asked, "Didn't you know I had to be in my Father's?" The word 'house' was added in many translations only to allow the sentence to make more sense. The parents wanted the child to go home with them. Yet Jesus had another home: he had one home in Nazareth, the other in heaven. He had two fathers: one was Joseph, Mary's husband, the other, God the Father. The two different homes were both calling out to him and, on that day, calling him in different directions.

We all have two homes: one on earth and one in God's Kingdom. Both are constantly calling us but sometimes in opposite directions. Both have expectations, attachments, and significant relationships we are called to attend to. As in Jesus' case, our two homes expect us to be in different places, to focus on different things, to see things from different perspectives, and to obey different masters. These conflicting pulling forces create spiritual, mental, and relational strains throughout our walk with God. The older we get, the more strains we notice and experience.

Jesus was not spared from these strains either. At the heart of the passage is the verb: 'to search' (or 'to look for' in NIV). It appears three times in verses 44-45 when Jesus' parents were searching for him, and is repeated twice in verses 48-49 in their dialogue. Luke highlights the verb a total of five times to emphasize Mary and Joseph's desperate act of searching for a lost son. Jesus' earthly home had to search for him while he was attending to another home. Jesus was at the centre of a tension created by the pulling forces between two worlds.

As we grow in the journey of life, we become aware that more and more people and things are seeking us out, imposing their expectations on us, calling us to be whom they want us to be. Meanwhile, carrying our cross to follow Jesus and living out God's calling means we are dealing with two homes: the earthly and the heavenly. We are called to take care of both homes and to submit to both in obedience. Easier said than done!

What magical formula would Jesus offer to resolve this conflict? Does the story provide any practical answer to the problem of juggling between the two worlds? No, not really. God did not remove the tension between the two worlds and the two identities for Jesus. The Bible tells us that, in the end, Jesus' parents still could not understand what was happening (verse 49), but they treasured these things in their hearts and continued to bring Jesus up as his earthly parents despite not understanding everything.

On the other hand, Jesus acknowledged the tension between his two homes, pointed out to his earthly father that he also had a heavenly Father to whom he needed to submit, and later chose to submit to his earthly parents by following them back home to Nazareth. Both Jesus and his parents chose to submit in obedience until the end.

In fact, Jesus is part of two intimate relationships. One was with his earthly family, the other within the Trinity. In the Christian faith, one of the biggest theological mysteries people are most baffled by is the concept of the Trinity. Our God is one, but also three persons at the same time. It is indeed beyond any level of human understanding and it is not my intention to solve this mystery here. The Bible does not explain a lot about the Trinity, at least not as much as we wish it had. However, the Bible constantly highlights two features of the Trinity. First, there is relationship within the Godhead. God does not need to create human beings to have relationships. The Trinity is the perfection of relationship.

The second aspect of the Trinity the Bible emphasizes in detail is that the Son totally submits to the Father's will, as if it is the one thing the Bible wants to make sure we know about the Trinity. Jesus' journey of submitting to the Father's will is a consistent theme throughout the four Gospels, and is also highlighted in various books in the Epistles. Evidently, this is what God wants us to learn. While relationships are the very essence of life, submission is the essence of a relationship. Submission is to lay down your own needs and desires for the sake of the other person. For a Christian to live a life without regret is to live a life in obedience to the Creator's calling. This is how we know we have lived our life to the full. Here in Luke

2, the story of Jesus staying behind in the temple of Jerusalem is one of the earliest physical demonstration of Jesus' submission to the Heavenly Father first.

If the Bible doesn't offer any magical formula for submission, then how did Jesus deal with it? The ending of the passage simply echoes the same simple summary about Jesus' early life:

> **50** Jesus grew in wisdom and stature, and in favour
> with God and man.

In other words, there was no quick fix. Jesus simply continued to grow, in the same pace and manner as a normal human would. To learn obedience is simply to learn it step by step as we grow. The verb 'grow' is repeated here to highlight it was a gradual process and journey. God's answer for us is not to abandon the earthly home, or to have answers to all our questions, but to grow in wisdom in Him as we continue to rely on Him amid different tensions in our lives. In James 1:5-6, God promises He is more than willing to give wisdom to us whenever we ask. If even Jesus needed wisdom, and if God gave it to him whenever he needed it, how much more do we need wisdom from God, and how much more does God want to give it to us?

Apart from growing in wisdom, another answer highlighted and repeated from verses 39-40 is grace. Although the NIV uses the word 'favour' in verse 50, the Greek word χάριτι actually means graciousness. Can you believe even Jesus needed grace? Grace is a free gift from someone else, not a result of ability or reward for hard work. Jesus needed grace when he was born, and his family certainly needed a lot of grace from God while bringing him up, especially while fleeing to Egypt from King Herod's massacre. We can be assured that God fully understands all the needs, struggles, and tensions throughout our lives as we juggle between conflicting demands and expectations. We are also promised that His grace is always sufficient for us, just as it was for Jesus.

When you look back to the early days of your life and your journey with God over the years, what do you see? Do you see your childhood as only a series of time-wasting wanderings and irrelevant events that have nothing to do with what God has called you to do? Or are you able to recognize God's presence and blessing in every tiny step throughout your life as you grow slowly in Him? When you face conflicting demands and strains from different realms of life, do you see God leaving you alone in your struggles to obey His calling? Or do you see God eagerly desiring to give you all the wisdom and grace you need in every small step of your walk with Him? In God's creation, nothing is wasted, and nothing is too insignificant.

Let's come to His throne of mercy with full confidence and learn to receive the wisdom and grace that He has already prepared for us to live out His calling.

2.

What do you want?

(John 1:35-51)

"What do you want?"

This was the first question Jesus asked after he started his ministry—at least we know it was the first question ever recorded according to the Gospel of John.

What exactly was Jesus talking about? And why did he ask such a question? Let's read the story in its full context in John 1:35-51.

35 The next day John was there again with two of his disciples. **36** When he saw Jesus passing by, he said, "Look, the Lamb of God!" **37** When the two disciples heard him say this, they followed Jesus. **38** Turning around, Jesus saw them following and asked, "What do you want?" They said, "Rabbi" (which means "Teacher"), "where are you staying?"

39 "Come," he replied, "and you will see." So they went and saw where he was staying, and they spent that day with him. It was about four in the afternoon. **40** Andrew, Simon Peter's brother, was one of the two who heard what John had said and who had followed Jesus. **41** The first thing Andrew did was to find his brother Simon and tell him, "We have found the Messiah" (that is, the Christ). **42** And he brought him to Jesus. Jesus looked at him and said, "You are Simon son of John. You will be called Cephas" (which, when translated, is Peter).

43 The next day Jesus decided to leave for Galilee. Finding Philip, he said to him, "Follow me." **44** Philip, like Andrew and Peter, was from the town of Bethsaida. **45** Philip found Nathanael and told him, "We have found the one Moses wrote about in the Law, and about whom the prophets also wrote—Jesus of Nazareth, the son of Joseph." **46** "Nazareth! Can anything good come from there?" Nathanael asked. "Come and see," said Philip. **47** When Jesus saw Nathanael approaching, he said of him, "Here truly is an Israelite in whom there is no deceit." **48** "How do you know me?" Nathanael asked. Jesus answered, "I saw you while you were still under the fig tree before Philip called you."

49 Then Nathanael declared, "Rabbi, you are the Son of God; you are the king of Israel." **50** Jesus said, "You believe because I told you I saw you under the fig tree. You will see greater things than that." **51** He then added, "Very truly I tell you, you will see 'heaven open, and the angels of God ascending and descending on the Son of Man."

As we read the story carefully, we see that Jesus wasn't asking the question to people who were still unsure about following him, but to those who *had already* started to follow him.

The Greek verb for 'want' that Jesus used here is ζητεῖτε (*zēteite*), which is a word that implies much more than simply wanting a thing. It is not the casual "What do you want?" question that a shop assistant asks when serving a customer, or a mother asking her children what they want for dinner. The word here has the same Greek root word used in Jesus' famous teaching, "But *seek* first the kingdom of God and his righteousness; and all these things will be given to you" (Matthew 6:33). It means to seek, to thrive for, and to go after a bigger long-term objective.

So Jesus' question could be paraphrased as, "What exactly are you going after when you're following me?". If Jesus asked his disciples this question, he was probably implying that even they themselves did not know what they were seeking.

Of course, Jesus knew what was in their hearts and minds. He knew everything, but he was deliberately asking this simple, obvious, yet significant question so that those who were following him would pause and think carefully. We all need to know what we are truly going after when we make the decision to follow Christ.

Let's go back to the story. The disciples answered by saying, "Rabbi, where are you staying?" (John 1:38).

The question "Where are you staying?" is not the type of question we ask today when we exchange phone numbers or email addresses with someone. In those days, to call someone 'Rabbi' meant you acknowledged that the person was a reputable teacher and leader in the community, so when the disciples asked a rabbi where he was staying, they were implying that they were willing to follow him and learn from him. Learning from Jesus involves staying with Jesus, literally.

This rabbi-follower relationship is much deeper than the teacher-student relationships we have in our modern society today. We do not live with our teachers, nor do we commit ourselves to imitating their way of life. Discipleship is not just about enrolling in a course to get a certificate or consulting an expert for some advice on a subject. It is a form of life-long apprenticeship. When you become a disciple of someone, you do not follow anyone else.

So how did Jesus reply to the disciples' question? He did not give them an address, but an invitation, "Come and see" (verse 39).

Did you notice the verb 'see' appears again and again throughout this story? But what was there to see? How did this relate to Jesus' first question, "What do you want?"

To 'see' requires us to be open-minded to whatever God wants to show us. As we continue to read, we might notice something strange. Despite the consistent emphasis on 'seeing', the author did not even bother to write about what they really saw. Imagine literally staying the night with Jesus! What would you want to see? His habits? How he says grace? What he wears? We might be interested in lots of details, but John did not seem to think these were important.

The next day, Andrew went to find his brother Simon (verse 40). The Bible tells us the first thing Andrew did was to tell Simon, "We have found the Messiah," and to bring Simon to Jesus. So, again, what exactly did Andrew see in Jesus the previous night that compelled him to reach this verdict? We are all curious to know. Again, Andrew did not explain what he had seen. He simply brought Simon to Jesus and let him see for himself.

Among our church circles, we often love hearing testimonies from other people about what they have seen or heard. We get that warm, fuzzy feeling when we hear happy stories and details of people's encounters with God which help us to feel closer to God. John's account here, however, is all about the invitation, "Come and see".

Verse 42 tells us about Simon's encounter: Jesus simply saw Simon and said, "You are Simon, son of John. You will be called Cephas."

In other words, John emphasized that it was Jesus who saw Simon, not the other way round. We cannot count on ourselves to 'see' God, but on God seeing us. Jesus called Simon by name, stated his history, and gave him a new name with a new identity. Jesus saw Simon's past, present, and future. Before we know Jesus, Jesus knows us. That is what the Gospel is about.

Being known by God is the most intimate, essential thing in life. Luke 13:25-30 and Matthew 7:21-23 give us one of the most horrifying warnings from Jesus: that in the end times, God will tell some people, "I never knew you. Away from me, you evildoers!" How sad is that?

But earlier in the same chapter in John, we learned that Jesus was with God even before the creation of the world: "In the beginning was the Word, [...] and the Word was God" (John 1:1). God knew you personally even since the very beginning. He sees our whole life in totality, gives us a new identity in Him, and calls us to a new life in Him. This is what we need to see.

Saint Augustine wrote in *Confessions*, "Let me know you, O you who know me; then shall I know even as I am known". In other words, the most important thing we need to know about God is that God knows us.

We all know that it is impossible for us to know God. I teach in a Bible school, and I can tell you that the people who study in Bible colleges or seminaries are those who understand this impossibility the most. The more we try to study God, the more we realize we cannot know God unless God shows Himself to us. If we rely on our own understanding to know God, it will be totally hopeless. But God knows us, and since the beginning, He has always been more than willing to make this connection possible.

Now let's get back to the story. The author then turns our attention to Philip and Nathanael, and the same pattern of seeing and being seen. Philip knew Jesus was the Messiah, but again we have no idea what Philip had really seen previously that had convinced him of this fact. However, Nathanael the sceptic disagreed, asking "Can anything good come from Nazareth?" (verse 46). Again, what Philip and Nathanael saw was not the most important. The most important was what Jesus saw.

Verse 47 says Jesus saw Nathanael and called him "an Israelite in whom there is no deceit."

"How do you know me?" Nathanael asked. Nathanael suddenly found himself asking a more personal question.

Jesus answered, "I saw you while you were still under the fig tree before Philip called you" (verse 48).

Then Nathanael declared, "Rabbi, you are the Son of God; you are the king of Israel."

What led to this sudden, dramatic 180-degree turn in Nathanael's attitude towards Jesus? What did Nathanael really see in that short and strange exchange? The answer is simple: he saw that Jesus could see through him.

Numerous scholars have tried to come up with all sorts of interpretations to explain Jesus' strange answer in verses 47-48. Of course, it was easy for Jesus to see that Nathanael was an Israelite. The name Israel originated from the story of Jacob, the deceitful man who wrestled with God. Yet instead of condemning Jacob, God chose to bless him and gave him the name 'Israel' (see Genesis 27). Jacob's life was full of deceit, but Jesus knew Nathanael was different. He saw his heart and his character.

Jesus' answer regarding the fig tree could potentially be a reference to a well-known passage in the book of Hosea:

> "I found Israel like grapes in the wilderness; I saw your fathers as the first fruits on the fig tree in its first season. But they went to Baal Peor, and separated themselves to that shame; They became an abomination like the thing they loved" (Hosea 9:10).

God saw the ancestors of the Israelites as fruits of the fig tree, but they ended up worshipping false gods and giving themselves to idols. Therefore, the phrase 'under the fig tree' could potentially mean remaining under sin.

Nonetheless, no one knows for sure today exactly what Jesus' answer in verses 47-48 truly meant. Only Jesus and Nathanael himself would have known. Perhaps it was an inside joke? No matter how we interpret Jesus' reply, one thing is obvious: it convincingly demonstrated to Nathanael that Jesus knew him very well, so well that he instantly switched from being a sceptic to a believer, proclaiming Jesus was the Messiah. He was transformed because he knew Jesus could see into his character and past experiences. He didn't see Jesus first; it was Jesus who saw him.

And Jesus wasn't finished. In verses 50-51, Jesus said he was going to show Nathanael and the other disciples much more:

> **50** "You will see greater things than that. **51** Very truly I tell you, you will see heaven open, and the angels of God ascending and descending on the Son of Man."

This time, anyone who knows Scripture well can tell where the reference came from: Genesis 28. It is about Jacob again. Jacob saw a vision of heaven opening, and the angels of God ascending and descending on a ladder (Genesis 28:12). This vision was one of the key affirmations of God's everlasting covenant and promises to Abraham, Isaac, Jacob and all of God's people. It was also an affirmation of God's presence remaining with Jacob, even after knowing all his sins. Here Jesus is saying, *"Not only can I see you, I will also fulfil God's everlasting covenant with you and through you."*

This is the true meaning of 'Calling'. Calling is not about finding what career suits you. It is about being known by God and knowing that He has created you, has seen everything in your past, present, and future, and has called you to be part of the fulfilment of what He has already promised.

In another story in the Gospels, Jesus also used the verb 'see' to explain our relationship with him. On one occasion, the Pharisees showed contempt for Jesus because he often spent time with sinners. Jesus responded with an analogy to explain his mission, "Those who are healthy have no need of a physician, but those who are sick" (Mark 2:17).

When we are sick, we often say we will "go and see a doctor". Actually, the whole point of seeing a doctor is not really to *see* the doctor, but to *be seen* by the doctor. It's not that you need to see the doctor, but you need the doctor to see you. The most important part is that the doctor sees you, sees any problems inside your body, and sees what treatments you may need. This is why the Gospels emphasize that God sees us.

Simon Peter later learned this valuable lesson. During Jesus' trials and crucifixion, Peter firmly denied he had any relationship with Jesus not only once, but three times, exactly as Jesus had predicted. He betrayed Jesus three times! But Jesus knew him, including both his prospects of failing as well as his new identity as the 'Rock' of the Church. That's what really matters.

The finale of John's Gospel ends with the amazing story of Jesus reinstating Peter after his denial. Three times Jesus asked Peter, "Do you love me?" (John 21:15-17). When reading this well-known story, Christians often focus on the word *agape*, the Greek word for love that Jesus had used. But let's also pay attention to what Peter said.

Peter didn't simply answer, "I love you", because, in reality, Peter had hopelessly failed to demonstrate that. Instead, Peter answered, "Lord, *you know* I love you." Peter knew Jesus knew. That was Peter's only hope. He had learned the crux of the Gospel: God knows us and still loves us, and He still uses us for His kingdom.

Today, Jesus is asking you the same question, "What do you want?" What exactly are you going after when you follow him? Well, come and see. See that God knows you and wants an everlasting relationship with you.

3.

What do you want me to do for you?

(Luke 18:35-43)

For many people, the loss of sight is the most feared disability. Yet have you ever imagined a blind person being able to see things more clearly than you can?

Here's a story of a blind man who not only could see more clearly than everyone else around him, but also helped others to see. How could that be possible? What can we learn from him? This story is found in Luke 18: 35-43.

35 As Jesus approached Jericho, a blind man was sitting by the roadside begging. **36** When he heard the crowd going by, he asked what was happening. **37** They told him, "Jesus of Nazareth is passing by." **38** He called out, "Jesus, Son of David, have mercy on me!" **39** Those who led the way rebuked him and told him to be quiet, but he shouted all the more, "Son of David, have mercy on me!" **40** Jesus stopped and ordered the man to be brought to him. When he came near, Jesus asked him, **41** "What do you want me to do for you?" "Lord, I want to see," he replied. **42** Jesus said to him, "Receive your sight; your faith has healed you." **43** Immediately he received his sight and followed Jesus, praising God. When all the people saw it, they also praised God.

This is a very short story indeed, not even 10 verses in Luke's Gospel, considering the staggering transformation it had brought to one man's life. The story began when a blind beggar on the side of the road started begging for the right thing from the right person. In doing so, he revealed multiple things he could see very clearly, which all those around him in the story had failed to see. How many of these things can you identify when reading the story?

Let's start with verses 35-36.

First, this man could see that something very significant was happening, and he knew he had to do whatever he could to find out what it was. For many among the crowd walking with Jesus, it was just an ordinary day with the rabbi, tagging along, listening to Jesus' talk about God's kingdom and heading home when it was time to go. But for this man, he could see that this could be the most significant moment in his life. He kept asking who was there until he got the answer.

After teaching in a Bible seminary for many years myself, I have learned to assess students not merely by how they answer questions, but by the kind of questions they ask. The quality of their questions reveals everything about where they are at intellectually, mentally, and spiritually. This blind man knew the right questions to ask. He was not just there physically; his heart was also present. His mind was sharp enough to allow him to see through things. Though he could not physically see, he focused wholeheartedly on his surroundings because he had to find out something of paramount importance to him: whether the person passing by was truly the one he had been longing for. He saw the opportunity of a lifetime.

Often, we are physically present in a place, but our hearts and minds are distracted by all kinds of things that are not important. We see things and people around us with our physical eyes, but mentally we are not seeing what is truly important to us. Sometimes we just need to close our eyes and ask, "What is really happening here? Who is here? What and whom should I focus on?"

The second thing this blind man managed to see more clearly than others was who Jesus was. Jesus was only passing by. You may wonder, "So what's the big deal?" To the blind man it meant everything because he knew who Jesus was. When he found out it was indeed Jesus who was passing by near him, he called out at the top of his voice, "Jesus, Son of David!" (verse 38).

He saw that Jesus was the 'Son of David', the Messiah God had promised to all the forefathers and prophets in His everlasting covenant with mankind. At the time of the story, how many people on the entire planet were able to recognize who Jesus was? Not many at all, certainly not most of the religious leaders at the time. Thousands upon thousands of people in Jesus' time, including high priests and experts in the Law, saw Jesus performing amazing miracles but still failed to see who Jesus was. Yet the blind man saw, and for him, there was absolutely no need for further proof as to whether Jesus was the one true Saviour.

He knew he must get hold of Jesus at all costs *right now*. That was the only thing that mattered in his whole life. He could not wait any longer and risk letting this precious moment slip away, so he kept shouting and shouting to catch Jesus' attention and to get to him. He would rather die than let go of the chance to speak to Jesus.

However, having access to Jesus doesn't always mean you know how to approach him. The third thing the blind man saw very clearly was his own needs and hopelessness. Such is the reality for a blind person. Every day when you wake up in the morning, what's the first thing you do? Go to the bathroom? Check your phone? Or make a cup of coffee? Actually, it's none of the above. The very first thing we all do each morning is to open our eyes and see. Imagine, every morning this blind man opened his eyes and there had been only total darkness. Every single morning, his first waking moment cruelly reminded him of the fact that he could not see.

But there was more. The fourth thing he could see was that he could only ask Jesus for one thing: mercy. His request posed a striking contrast to the arrogant requests of some of the disciples to sit at Jesus' side when Jesus came into his kingdom (Mark 10: 35–45). Mercy is the only thing a sinner can ask for in front of the Creator and Saviour. We are not worthy to ask for anything or earn anything from God. Yet how many of us can see that Jesus' mercy is our only hope?

Jesus was often served and helped by his followers. I bet many of those people were thinking that they were the ones serving Jesus' needs. Very few of us can see that we are the ones in desperate need of Jesus' mercy. The man could clearly see that his only way out of his hopeless situation was through putting his hope in Jesus, not in himself. He saw the essence of the Gospel.

What was Jesus' response? Jesus asked him a question that seemed rather redundant, "What do you want me to do for you?" The man had already been shouting repeatedly to Jesus, "Have mercy on me!" But Jesus still had to ask him to clarify what exactly he meant by that.

Again, without hesitation, the man gave an answer that could not have been more precise: "I want to see." What would you say if you were him? He's a beggar, so naturally a beggar would say something like, "Sir, please spare some change," unless he knew the person in front of him was no ordinary person.

If you knew the one asking you the question was your Creator, your Saviour, and your God, you would answer accordingly. Your answer would reveal how much you know about yourself, your real needs, and the power of your Saviour. The most important question is whether we really know what our real needs are.

At the seminary where I teach, there was a student who was always ill. How can you help a student who is always calling in sick for class? What do you think his greatest need was? Did he need to go and see a doctor? No, he was unwell because he was too stressed. But why was he so stressed? Well, he couldn't cope with the assignments. And why couldn't he cope? Later, after we talked to him to dig deeper into his life, we found out that he had been avoiding his assignments. So why was he doing that? At last, we discovered that due to some childhood issues, he couldn't accept any failure in his life. What, then, do you think this student needed most?

We as humans only like to focus on our superficial wants and desires. We hardly ever see our own deepest needs underneath all the facades. We all need God to open our eyes to see what we truly need. As far as God is concerned, we are all blind and hopeless, unless He opens our eyes.

Jesus' question, "What do you want me to do for you?" was not just a casual, rhetorical question. It established a relationship. It was God making a personal offer to a desperate seeker. The question, "What do you want me to do for you?" was God's blank cheque, payable to you, signed with God's own signature. You just need to decide what you want to ask from God and write it on the cheque. It was indeed an invitation from Jesus himself: "Just ask, and I will give you what you really need!"

If Jesus asks you today, "What do you want me to do for you?" how would you answer? Do you know what you truly need from Jesus? The reason why we don't know is because we are too busy focusing on things we don't really need, things that distract us from seeing the truly important things in life. The blind man didn't have the distractions we have.

In verse 42, Jesus gave him exactly what he asked for, "Receive your sight; your faith has healed you." Imagine that the first sight he saw with his eyes was the face of Jesus!

When reading an eyewitness account of a blind man being healed, we might expect the author to put a lot of emphasis on the idea of 'seeing'. Yet surprisingly, Luke hardly used the verb 'see' throughout the original text. Instead, Jesus said, "Receive your sight." It was like Jesus was saying to him, "As long as you recognize your needs, you can just ask me and receive."

Just like the blind man, we might not have seen God's miracles directly with our own eyes, but can we believe like this blind man did, with a pure, focused, innocent faith? He had only heard about Jesus, but he could see very clearly that Jesus was the promised Saviour he must seek after. He was so confident that he was able to ignore the rebukes of all the people around him. Faith is seeing, just as the author of Hebrews wrote in Hebrews 11:1, "Faith is seeing what is invisible to the naked eye."

Have you ever thought that blindness and faith often go together? What kind of people do you think have the most opportunities to exercise their faith? I believe it is the people who are blind.

I remember a blind person who once told me that the biggest lesson he had had to learn after becoming blind was to have faith in people. In everything he did, he needed someone to lead and guide him. He had no choice but to believe that other people were really helping him and not going to harm him. When he was asked to sit down, he had to believe the chair behind him was able to hold him. He couldn't see anything, so he had to trust people even in the smallest details of life.

On my way home from work, I often see a blind man commuting on the same bus route. He can cross the road according to the sounds he hears, and he can get to the bus stop easily with the help of his cane. However, after arriving at the bus stop, he can only rely on other people at the bus stop to tell him the number of the bus arriving, and he has to believe that the person is telling him the truth, otherwise he would never make it onto the bus. Are we any different from this man in our walk with God? When it comes to things we cannot see, our only way out is to have faith.

We sometimes use the expression 'blind faith' to refer to superstitions or beliefs that have no scientific basis. In reality, life itself is a faith exercise. What our naked eyes can see is very limited, especially when it comes to things beyond human understanding. We have to believe in Jesus and look up to him because the eyes of faith are the brightest. We have to admit that out in the realms of life that are beyond our control, we are all blind, and that faith is the only way out. The blind man could "see" Jesus because he didn't have hope in seeing anything else, and this faith saved him.

Who, then, is the blind one in the story? The people who rebuked the blind man for crying out to Jesus were totally blind to the wonders God had planned for that day. Ironically, at the end of the story, they were the ones who had to be led by the blind man. Verse 43 tells us that "immediately he received his sight and followed Jesus, praising God. When all the people saw it, they also praised God."

This verse poses a stark contrast to the beginning of the story. At first, the blind man was sitting by the roadside; now he is praising God. Before he was being silenced by the people; now he is helping the people to see. Before, he was begging; now he is leading the people in glorifying God. An alternative definition of the word 'glory' is 'visible goodness'. When we see God, we lead other people around us to see the visible goodness of God.

People who have experienced extreme helplessness can appreciate God's grace and work far better than others can. Those who have not experienced major difficulties in life often believe that they can rely on themselves; their self-reliance blinds them from seeing God's grace. When a blind man sees the grace of God, he not only sees its power but also the depth of God's glory. In turn, such insight helps others to see the beauty of God's glory too.

May we all be able to see what the blind man saw, and may God open our eyes so that we can also help those around us see God's work and glory.

4.

Do you want to get well?

(John 5:1-18)

When we look at all the questions Jesus asked throughout his ministry as recorded in the four Gospels, we see that some of his questions are fundamentally important, such as, "Who do you say I am?", which he asked his closest disciples when they were alone (Mark 8:27). Yet some of Jesus' questions were rather awkward or puzzling to the people around him; some were highly provocative and controversial, especially those posed to the religious leaders; and some seemed rather redundant and even laughable.

One example of a seemingly pointless question is recorded in John 5:1-9, the famous story of the 'Healing at the Pool'. Let's look at the intriguing conversation that took place between Jesus and a sick man.

> **1** Some time later, Jesus went up to Jerusalem for one of the Jewish festivals. **2** Now there is in Jerusalem near the Sheep Gate a pool, which in Aramaic is called Bethesda and which is surrounded by five covered colonnades. **3** Here a great number of disabled people used to lie—the blind, the lame, the paralyzed. **5** One who was there had been an

invalid for thirty-eight years. **6** When Jesus saw him lying there and learned that he had been in this condition for a long time, he asked him, "Do you want to get well?"

7 "Sir," the invalid replied, "I have no one to help me into the pool when the water is stirred. While I am trying to get in, someone else goes down ahead of me."

8 Then Jesus said to him, "Get up! Pick up your mat and walk." **9** At once the man was cured; he picked up his mat and walked. The day on which this took place was a Sabbath, **10** and so the Jewish leaders said to the man who had been healed, "It is the Sabbath; the law forbids you to carry your mat."

11 But he replied, "The man who made me well said to me, 'Pick up your mat and walk.' "

12 So they asked him, "Who is this fellow who told you to pick it up and walk?"

13 The man who was healed had no idea who it was, for Jesus had slipped away into the crowd that was there.

14 Later Jesus found him at the temple and said to him, "See, you are well again. Stop sinning or something worse may happen to you." **15** The man went away and told the Jewish leaders that it was Jesus who had made him well.

16 So, because Jesus was doing these things on the Sabbath, the Jewish leaders began to persecute him. **17** In his defense Jesus said to them, "My Father is always at his work to this very day, and I too am working." **18** For this reason they tried all the more to kill him; not only was he breaking the Sabbath, but he was even calling God his own Father, making himself equal with God.

Jesus was asking a person who was ill if he wanted to be healed. If you were the sick man, you would probably be thinking, "Does this even need to be asked? If I don't want to be well again, what am I doing here all day?!"

If you're familiar with the four Gospels, you will have noticed that almost all of the cases of Jesus' healing started when the people suffering from illnesses overcame huge obstacles to come before Jesus to ask him for healing, or at least had a family member or friend who sought Jesus' help on his or her behalf. Jesus hardly ever took the initiative to heal people. Getting everyone physically healed was not Jesus' priority in his mission on earth. Moreover, if he had focused on healing all the sick people, it would have only stirred up inappropriate responses from the crowd and hinder his true mission.

But this time, it was an exception. The man did not seek Jesus' help. It was Jesus who took the initiative to ask this man if he wanted to be healed. His question was like asking, "Will you let me heal you?"

What was so special about this man? And what do we know about him? Verse 5 tells us that this man had been sick for 38 years! However, the saddest thing was that he had no fighting spirit. Some manuscripts added that this man was waiting for the water to move because "whoever went down first would be healed" (5:3-4). If this was the case, then everyone would eagerly get ready to jump into the pool as soon as possible, but this man sounded like he couldn't be bothered.

Jesus' question wasn't a simple one. It wasn't only about the possibility of healing, but also the hope of healing—and this hope could only come from God.

Many people give up on themselves because they cannot see a way out, but the way out can only be found in God. It requires allowing God to help you, which, surprisingly, can be the most difficult step for many people. Jesus asked this strange but necessary question to rekindle hope for this man. To say to Jesus, "Yes, I do want to be healed" would imply a willingness to let go of all the methods he had always relied on and to depend solely on him.

But how did this man answer Jesus' question? You might expect the answer to be something like, "Of course! Since you are here, please help me go down to the pool when the water moves!" But instead, he said, "Sir, no one put me in the pool when the water was moving; when I was going, someone else went down before me" (verse 7).

He didn't really answer Jesus' question, did he? Here's an answer full of despair, resentment, and hopelessness. What he really meant was, "Even if someone helps me, it won't be fast enough anyway, so it's just pointless."

We could laugh at this man or pity him for not knowing who he was talking to, but perhaps he knew and had simply lost all hope. Even when Jesus approached him with the offer of healing, he simply avoided the question.

What was the problem? The story tells us that the people sitting around the pool were either blind, lame, or withered (verse 3). In other words, they were the kind of people who couldn't get to the pool by themselves. So this man wasn't alone, but what made him different was that he couldn't see any possibility of change. That was the crux of the problem.

However, if he had really given up hope, why was he still sitting there by the pool? Was it because he was still hoping something would happen one day? Or perhaps he didn't know where else he could go other than the same spot he had been lying in for the last 38 years?

It's hard for us to imagine that a person would wait 38 years for one thing to happen to change his fate. 38 years of futile waiting is long enough to destroy anyone's remaining hope. The man's answer showed that he was used to this status quo of despair. For him, being hopeless was normal.

His answer to Jesus also included a logical explanation. His mind, wired to process life through the lens of despair, came up with a good excuse to rationalize his current situation: no one could help him down into the pool. That's it. He had determined to remain in this same position for the rest of his life. It didn't matter at all. This was the most tragic part of his answer.

The author John didn't explain what disease this man was suffering from, and it doesn't matter. Maybe he was indeed paralyzed, but his true paralysis was that of the soul. He needed Jesus to ask him, "Do you want to be healed?" because he couldn't even ask Jesus himself when Jesus was literally standing in front of him. He was that hopeless — a staggering contrast from the blind beggar who continually cried out from the top of his voice, "Son of David, have mercy on me!" (Luke 18:35-43).

So what could make a person as miserable as this? He had a fixed belief about his problem and what the solution should be. His excuse revealed how strongly he insisted that he had to be the first person to jump into this pool. In his mind, he could only be healed by one particular method, and not even Jesus could do anything about it. Yet his method was neither realistic nor suitable for him, because he could never be the first person to go down.

As a result, 38 years had passed and he was still there. It had become his 'identity'. The mental trap he had set for himself defined who he was.

What was Jesus' take on this situation? In verse 8, Jesus said to him, "Get up, take your mat and go!" It was a very simple command, which contained three actions: get up, pick up, and go.

To appreciate the healing Jesus offered to this man, we must first understand a verb that was emphasized by the author three times in the original text: the word 'to have', although this emphasis isn't clearly shown in many modern Bible translations.

In the original Greek text, in verse 2, the phrase "surrounded by five covered colonnades" contains an emphasis on the verb 'to have'. It was deliberately used by the author to express that the sick people had a place enclosed by those five colonnades where they could stay.

In verse 5, it says, "There was someone who was sick for thirty-eight years." The author used the verb 'to have' to highlight the man's situation. The original verse can be translated literally as: "In him, he has 38 years of illness", though many of our Bible translations today have omitted the verb chosen by the author.

In verse 7, the original text also uses the same verb: "I have no one to put me in the pool." So, in total, the author used 'to have' three times in the story:

1. The sick people 'had' a place for shelter.
2. He 'had' a 38-year-old disease.
3. He 'had' no one to put him in the pool.

Scripture points out that this man 'had' three things: a disease, which rendered him totally disabled for many years; a place which served as a comfort zone for him to hide in; and an excuse, which allowed him to settle for the status quo. These were three mental traps which had essentially defined the man's identity and fate.

Do we have any similar mental traps in our lives that have been shaping who we are and preventing us from seeing the possibility of change? These mental traps can be conscious or subconscious. Do we creatively come up with a false comfort zone where our excuses for our despondency makes sense to us, and do we stubbornly fix our eyes on only one human solution? What is the 'pool' in your life where you are hoping other people will carry you so that you can be 'healed' through your own method?

Now let's turn to Jesus' answer. The three actions in Jesus' command precisely targeted these three issues the man was 'having'. First, regarding the man having a sickness for 38 years, Jesus told him to "get up"; he was already healed because Jesus had healed him. Second, regarding having the five colonnades as his secure hiding place, Jesus told him to "take up your mat"; he no longer belonged to this place, so there was no point in him staying and lingering there anymore. Finally, in response to his excuse of having no one to put him in the pool, Jesus said, "Let's go." The sick man's own method of healing could now be dismissed, and he no longer needed to wait for false salvation from other people.

The man obeyed Jesus' command immediately and he got up! However, there was one major obstacle. This time it wasn't a physical problem, but a social and religious obstacle: Jesus gave the command on a Sabbath! According to Jewish religious traditions and regulations, people were not allowed to do any type of work, including carrying any weight, during the Sabbath. So this man was not supposed to carry his mat, which would definitely be considered a heavy weight according to the Pharisees.

Couldn't Jesus have come just a little bit earlier, or a day later? Did this healing have to take place during this particular day at this inconvenient hour? The man had been like this for 38 years anyway, so what difference would it have made if he had waited for one more day? Perhaps Jesus could have instructed the man to go and enjoy his weekend first, then come back to dispose of his mat later? No one would give him a parking ticket during the Sabbath, right? The story could have been concluded with a happily-ever-after ending. But things are never this simple when Jesus is involved in our lives.

Yes, Jesus wanted the man to follow his commands right now. Following Jesus and doing God's will is for right now, not for later. Indeed, it was Jesus himself who offered the healing. How is this related to the Sabbath?

The Sabbath was never only about taking some time off from work. That was the Pharisees' understanding. Nor is it a friendly reminder for us to relax on a Sunday afternoon, as many modern Christians tend to think. It's all about the holy fulfilment of God's work and purposes on earth. It's a command to stop focusing on work itself and to direct our focus on the one who truly fulfils and accomplishes the meaning of all work. God is not just the Alpha; He is also the Omega. The Sabbath is about honouring the Omega. This is what true rest is about: finding our ultimate fulfilment and satisfaction in God. We don't look elsewhere.

In the Old Testament, the order of fallow in the Jubilee year (Leviticus 25:8-12) was not really for environmental protection, and the order to not pick up any manna on the Sabbath while God's people were in the wilderness (Exodus 16:19-36) wasn't about taking a break, although these reasons may also be part of God's will. The real lesson was to trust God to provide more than enough rather than to trust in our own methods to protect ourselves. God authorized the rest from farming and gathering food because He is the one in charge of the provision.

In the New Testament, one well-known Bible passage about rest is Jesus' analogy in Matthew chapter 11:

> **28** "Come to me, all you who are weary and burdened, and I will give you rest. **29** Take my yoke upon you and learn from me, for I am gentle and humble in heart, and you will find rest for your souls. **30** For my yoke is easy and my burden is light."

Notice the ox wears the yoke only when it is working. So the 'yoke' is for work, not for taking a break. Nevertheless, for many of us, work and rest seem like a contradiction, especially if we have a very narrow definition of work and rest. However, they are not contradictory when we're working in the way God has ordained. Jesus said, "Take my yoke" (i.e., take off your old yoke), because his way of working is easy. Work is about doing things his way, not yours.

Therefore, the Sabbath is all about God's authority and sovereignty. Only God, as the one who decides the purpose and meaning of life, has the authority to decide how the Sabbath is to be defined and lived out, because the Sabbath is all about the fulfilment of His purpose, will, and plan. Both Jesus and the offended religious leaders knew very well about this serious implication. This was why John dedicated a large part of the chapter to discussing the Sabbath and authority after the man was healed.

In verses 10-11, when the religious leaders criticized the man for carrying his mat (i.e., for not following their narrow interpretation of the Sabbath), the man simply replied, "The man who made me well said to me, 'Pick up your mat and walk.'"

As far as this man was concerned, whoever had healed him had the authority to tell him what to do on the Sabbath. Although, according to John's narratives, this man sadly didn't seem to have much knowledge of or interest in Jesus, he still knew better than the religious leaders when it came to who had more authority on the Sabbath!

The Sabbath is holy, not because it is a day off, but because it's about remembering God is the one who fulfils His work, not us. On this particular Sabbath, God decided to offer healing to this man. He liberated him from all of the physical and mental constraints he had been living under for decades and redefined his whole life. There was no better way to honour the Sabbath than to accept God's offer by the power of God's Son: to get up, pick up the mat and walk.

Is Jesus asking you to pick up any 'mat' today? The act of picking up your 'mat' on the Sabbath has multiple profound meanings. It means you accept Jesus' authority over you. It means you are giving up your own method of self-rescuing. It means you are revoking your old excuses or self-justification. It means you are not relying on others to put you in the 'pool'. It also means you are breaking the rules established by those who claim to know what God can or cannot do in your life. Finally, it means you are giving an account to share with the world what Jesus has done in your life.

5.

Why all this commotion and wailing?

(Mark 5:22-24, 35-43)

You are at the funeral of a child who has just died from immense suffering. The coffin is surrounded by devastated, grieving family members and friends. All you can hear is sobbing, moaning, wailing. Your heart sank as you wordlessly stood among the broken-hearted.

Suddenly, someone from the crowd raised his voice, "Why all this commotion and wailing?" All heads turn to the direction of the voice. Everyone is trying to find out who just asked such a ridiculous question. What would be your reaction? What is wrong with this person? Either he is the rudest and most insensitive person in the world, or he simply has no idea what is happening.

Or maybe he is the only one who knows what is actually happening.

Our lives are full of commotion and wailing. We go through struggles, sickness, disappointments, failures, and the deaths of loved ones. Why all this commotion and wailing?

Here in Hong Kong, it has been recognized that there are three main 'pandemics' among the dwellers of the city. The first one is addiction. We are addicted to anything and everything.

We can see addiction even among very young children who are glued to the screen. Many of us are addicted to the internet, gaming, alcohol, sex, relationships, gambling, and money. You name it, we have it. Addiction is all about misplacing our love in the wrong place. We choose not to direct our love towards a living God, but at something that is dead and less satisfying instead.

The second pandemic is anxiety. We fear not being good enough, and we fear missing out. So every day, everything we do is all about chasing something that never satisfies, and we fear that we can't get what we think we deserve. As a result, we're driven by these desires, like walking zombies. Anxiety is realizing that what you're tightly holding onto is not reliable after all, but you're refusing to let it go because you don't know what else you can hold onto.

The third pandemic is depression. We see that the average age of people committing suicide is getting lower each year. Suicide is the direct product of a sheer, overwhelming sense of hopelessness and despair.

When you put all three together, you'll see we're living a life that only brings us painful, never-ending desperation for things that we can't let go of. Is there any way out from this hopeless human problem? Jesus and his resurrection are the ultimate answer. In Jesus, we see how the most hopeless, most horrible situations in life are turned around completely, in Jesus' own way and timing.

JESUS' AWKWARD QUESTIONS

This is the story of a father who is losing his beloved daughter to illness. Mark records the story in interesting detail. After healing a demon-possessed man by a lake, Jesus went on to cross the water while a large crowd of people followed him. Let's read Mark 5, starting from verse 22.

> **22** Then one of the synagogue leaders, named Jairus, came, and when he saw Jesus, he fell at his feet. **23** He pleaded earnestly with him, "My little daughter is dying. Please come and put your hands on her so that she will be healed and live." **24** So Jesus went with him. A large crowd followed and pressed around him.

Mark identified the main character of the story as a synagogue leader named Jairus. Indeed, it could be controversial for a religious leader to come to Jesus and ask for his help in public. Yet we know Jairus not only came to Jesus, but he even fell at his feet. He was in a desperate situation that's every parent's worst nightmare: witnessing your own child suffering and dying while nothing can be done. Mark emphasized that he 'pleaded earnestly' with Jesus (verse 23), and Jesus agreed to help him.

Then came an unexpected twist in the story. A woman who had been suffering bleeding for years happened to have chosen this very inconvenient time to come to Jesus for help, delaying Jesus' journey at this critical moment. The delay was probably expected by Jesus, but it surely wasn't in Jairus' plan. The clock was ticking, and time was running out for saving his daughter's life.

We'll look more closely at this woman's encounter with Jesus in another time. Let's focus on Jairus' desperate situation and skip to verse 35 for the rest of the story.

35 While Jesus was still speaking, some people came from the house of Jairus, the synagogue leader. "Your daughter is dead," they said. "Why bother the teacher anymore?" **36** Overhearing what they said, Jesus told him, "Don't be afraid; just believe." **37** He did not let anyone follow him except Peter, James and John the brother of James. **38** When they came to the home of the synagogue leader, Jesus saw a commotion, with people crying and wailing loudly.

39 He went in and said to them, "Why all this commotion and wailing? The child is not dead but asleep." **40** But they laughed at him. After he put them all out, he took the child's father and mother and the disciples who were with him, and went in where the child was. **41** He took her by the hand and said to her, "Talitha koum!" (which means "Little girl, I say to you, get up!"). **42** Immediately the girl stood up and began to walk around (she was twelve years old). At this they were completely astonished. **43** He gave strict orders not to let anyone know about this, and told them to give her something to eat.

Jesus said three things throughout the story. The first was when Jairus' worst nightmare came true. Someone from his house travelled all the way to find them and announced the death of his daughter. Jesus' response was, "Don't be afraid. Just believe."

We're afraid because we don't believe. Fear is the direct antithesis of faith. The two are constantly at odds. The antidote to fear is not finding a solution to our problem, but simply in believing. But believing in what?

Jairus believed in Jesus, didn't he? We can't deny the fact that he had faith in Jesus. That's why he came to Jesus and pleaded with him for help. He probably had more faith in Jesus than a lot of people of his time did.

But Jairus was still afraid. Well, of course, his daughter was literally dying! He feared Jesus wouldn't make it in time, and his worst fear came true! Jesus was indeed delayed by this woman who came out of nowhere. This woman had already been sick for so many years. Couldn't she wait for another couple of hours? Couldn't Jesus see there was a different priority of needs here? Or had Jairus' faith in Jesus been misplaced?

What do we fear today, and why? We fear whenever we can't hold onto something very dear to us, or if there's something we can't fully control. Jairus was a leader who had many things under his control, but he knew he had no control of Jesus' timing. He had no control over the woman who suddenly delayed Jesus' journey, and he certainly had no control over his daughter's life and death. His worst fear was confirmed when someone announced, *"It's too late"*.

Fear and faith are in fact two sides of the same coin. This is why Jesus said, "Don't be afraid. Just believe." What we fear most is what we believe in most. Our fears expose our deepest beliefs. Jairus was banking on Jesus' hurrying and making it to his home in time to heal the child. That's what he believed in, and that's what his greatest fears were all about. What we're afraid of exposes where our ultimate sense of security lies.

We all have fears and anxieties in each stage of our lives. When we're students, we worry. When we're looking for a job, we worry. When we've finally found a job, we still worry. When we're single, we worry. When we're getting married, we worry. After we're married, we still worry. Deep in our hearts we know nothing is reliable. We fear losing our jobs because we rely on them. Jesus' answer is not to secure what we want, but to help us look more clearly at what we fear and what we believe. When we realize what we're relying on is not reliable, we fear. The only way out is to let it go and find something or someone who is truly reliable to take its place.

Some people say religion is only for weak people who feel like they have no control over their own lives. Well, I'd like to ask these sceptics how much control they themselves really have over anything. I know of a doctor who went hiking with his colleagues. In the middle of the hike, he suddenly fell ill and had a heart attack. Guess what? He was literally surrounded by doctors. But no one could save him, and he sadly passed away in front of all his doctor friends. We have no control at all over what happens to us. Jairus was a synagogue leader who should have had it all. Yet he knew he still needed to come before the feet of Jesus and plead earnestly. Even after Jesus agreed to go and see his daughter, things were still out of his control. Jesus' message for him was simple: change what you fear and what you believe.

The second thing Jesus said was rather awkward, almost rude, when he arrived at the scene: "Why all this commotion and wailing? The child is not dead but asleep" (verse 39). Jesus' answer to the issue at hand was not at all what we'd expect. He didn't apologize for being late, for in God's timing there is no such thing as being 'too late'. Jesus offered a totally different perspective on death: the child was only sleeping. Only the one who has power over life and death could offer such a perspective.

Death is the most powerful and unwelcome reality every single human being needs to face at some point in life. It is also the ultimate consequence of our sin and broken relationship with the living God. It's Satan's most fearsome weapon. Where have we seen death's most insidious moment and threat in all of human history? It was on a day called Good Friday, when the Lord of Life was nailed to the cross and died. That was what seemed to be Satan's greatest display of power.

But that was it. It lasted less than 72 hours. Jesus rose again and death was defeated, forever. Now we can stare death in the eye and ask, "Death, where is your sting?" (1 Corinthians 15:55).

I know a friend who used to enjoy playing with bees when he was a young child. Children can be fearless, you know. He loved toying with bees and even allowed them to sting him. He didn't mind bee stings at all. Once the bees had tried to sting him, they immediately lost their sting and became harmless just like flies. This is what God has done to death for us. Death, where is your sting? Jesus said that whoever is in Him no longer needs to fear death, and once you have this victory that Jesus has won on the cross and from the empty tomb, what else need you fear?

The third thing Jesus said was in verse 41. Jesus said to the girl, "*Talitha koum!*" Why did Mark (and many Bible translators) choose to record this exact phrase in the text? In the original text, the phrase was a very casual expression, almost like a mother calling her daughter to get out of bed to go to school. The expression was a huge contrast to what Jairus was asking Jesus to do. In the story, Jairus had everything planned for Jesus: Jesus would go and formally lay hands on his daughter so that she would be healed.

Jesus didn't follow Jairus' plan. First, Jesus was late—he was *too* late. He should have arrived on time according to Jairus' script. Second, Jesus did not treat the girl as a patient to be healed, like Jairus had in mind. Instead, Jesus treated her like a sleeping girl to be woken up.

God never follows any human script. His way and timing are never the same as ours. This is not to scare us or to play with our emotions. Our own fears and limitations play with our emotions. We need a God who transcends all human understanding if we are to know Him and draw close to Him. We need to hear Jesus calling, "Talitha koum!"

Our human nature compels us to search for solutions, solve mysteries, and find explanations. When Jesus said, "It is finished," God provided the only and ultimate solution to all our quests and problems, so that we can be saved and live. Throughout human history, no one else has ever offered any better answer to death, or a better way to defeat addiction, anxiety, depression, or any other plague of the human soul. We just need to lay our trust and fear on the One who alone is worthy of our trust and fear.

6.

Who touched my clothes?

(Mark 5:25-34)

Jesus sometimes had a reputation for asking rather strange and puzzling questions, but there were only a few times in the Bible when even his disciples couldn't help but comment on how odd they thought his questions were. One example was the question: "Who touched my clothes?"—an apparently silly question that totally turned a life around forever.

Let's dive into the story in Mark 5:25-34:

25 A woman was there who had been subject to bleeding for twelve years. **26** She had suffered a great deal under the care of many doctors and had spent all she had, yet instead of getting better she grew worse. **27** When she heard about Jesus, she came up behind him in the crowd and touched his cloak, **28** because she thought, "If I just touch his clothes, I will be healed." **29** Immediately her bleeding stopped and she felt in her body that she was freed from her suffering. **30** At once Jesus realized that power had gone out from him. He turned around in the crowd and asked, "Who touched my clothes?" **31** "You see the people crowding against you," his disciples answered, "and yet you can ask, 'Who touched me?'" **32** But Jesus kept looking around to see who had done it. **33** Then the woman, knowing what had happened to her, came and fell at his feet and, trembling with fear, told him the whole truth. **34** He said to her, "Daughter, your faith has healed you. Go in peace and be freed from your suffering."

Modern readers with a scientific mind might like to speculate what disease the woman was suffering from and what treatment could have healed her today. But that's not the concern of the author. The text puts emphasis on how long and painful her suffering had been—twelve years! She had wasted and lost all her resources, time, and hope on doctors, and still nothing had improved. Each doctor's visit led to more disappointment and plunged her into deeper despair. Twelve years with doctors only proved to her that the bleeding was incurable.

Please note that we are not just talking about having anaemia here. We're talking about being 'unclean' in the eyes of everyone around her in her social context. The continuous bleeding meant that this woman was forever cut off from society, excluded from all forms of religious worship and social events. And since her condition was incurable, this wasn't like other forms of 'uncleanliness' specified in the Mosaic Law, under which people could wait for a period of time and be 'cleansed' by going through certain religious rituals, and later reintegrate into society. No, that wasn't the case for this woman.

Imagine being under strict quarantine for twelve years straight and knowing it will continue every single day until you die. This woman couldn't be near anyone; she was deprived of any physical touch, or else any person she came into contact with would also be considered unclean and suffer the exact same fate. She literally could not be near any living person. The bleeding meant a loss of all friends and family, and all forms of support networks a person would need to survive. In her world, there was no honour, only shame.

However, we know this woman believed in Jesus. At least, she believed Jesus was her last resort, and had quite a lot of confidence in Jesus' ability to heal her incurable disease. Sadly, even with her faith in Jesus, there were still an awful number of obstacles to overcome just to seek help from him. She couldn't walk near anyone or physically touch anyone, let alone speak to a highly respected rabbi in public! Any normal way of seeking help from a rabbi, or any usual way of approaching Jesus while he was teaching or eating with people, would be absolutely impossible for her.

So she came up with a masterplan for seeking help from Jesus: she would secretly and briefly touch a corner of Jesus' clothing. If no one noticed, she thought to herself, especially if Jesus didn't notice, then it would be fine! She only wanted her bleeding stopped. There was no need for Jesus to waste his time dealing with any other area of her life, right? So just a tiny, sneaky touch of his clothes would do. Then she could get on with her life and Jesus would get on with his, and no one would ever know that an unclean woman had touched Jesus. One stone kills many birds in her situation.

We can say this woman was pretty much cheating her way to Jesus. Her plan was surely not in line with the Law of Moses and the religious customs of her time. She made up her own method, her own script, and her own theology. But who can blame her? What else could she do? She simply had no other hope in the whole universe. Have you ever been in a situation when you saw absolutely no hope, only shame? If you have, you'd probably understand this woman's situation.

This woman had faith in Jesus and the determination to sneak up to him in secret, but the stakes were still very high. She must be very careful in reaching Jesus totally undetected among a huge moving crowd, most of whom knew the Law of Moses very well. Remember, a person with a bleeding medical condition has very little strength and could faint in an environment of little oxygen, especially in a crowded place.

But with God, she was never hopeless.

The day had come. The timing could not have been worse (or better, depending on whether you are looking at it from God's or our perspective). This story, as we saw in the previous chapter, was sandwiched right between Jairus' dramatic attempt to bring Jesus to his home to heal his dying daughter and the time when the servant announced that Jesus was 'too late' to save her.

The contrast between Jairus and this woman could not have been bigger. Jairus was a socially, religiously, possibly also politically, respected figure. He had easy access to Jesus and could speak to him in public any day. When he suddenly interrupted Jesus' teaching and requested him to visit his home to lay hands on his daughter (a grand gesture for a rabbi), no one seemed to question his right to do so.

The woman, however, was exactly the opposite of Jairus. Interrupting Jesus was the one thing she had to avoid at all costs in her plan. Her every single move and intention had to be kept in the dark because of her uncleanliness. This was why she only aimed to touch just a corner of Jesus' clothing, and it had to be without the knowledge of Jesus, or so she thought.

Surprisingly, Jairus and the woman also shared several things in common, apart from their desperate needs and their faith in Jesus' power to heal. First, they both came to Jesus with their own plans for how Jesus' healing would happen. They both seemed to know what was 'best' for Jesus and for themselves. Jairus' plan was to go and ask Jesus to follow him home on time in order to lay his hands on his daughter so that she could be healed. The woman's plan was to sneak up to Jesus, touch his clothes and be healed without being noticed.

Second, both their plans went horribly wrong as Jesus didn't follow their script. Jairus' plan depended on Jesus being on time. Yet Jesus suddenly decided to 'waste' time at the most critical moment by seeking out the woman and chatting with her, while allowing his journey to save his precious daughter to be delayed. And the girl died during this delay! For the woman, her operation was all about secrecy and privacy. Yet Jesus noticed something had happened and was determined to ask who had touched his clothes, in front of everybody, pausing his journey until he drew the woman out from the crowd.

Perhaps Jesus deliberately wanted to show Jairus how this woman's secretive method of sneaking her way in to seek Jesus' help could also work? I'm not suggesting we should come up with sneaky plans to get God's help or healing. God can heal and help anyone in any way He wishes. This is something beyond our comprehension, because we don't have the capacity to help and reach out to everyone around us. At the most extreme end of human desperation, like in this woman's case, we can do absolutely nothing except reach out to God as our last resort, even in ways that we know are hopeless by human standards, but the story demonstrates that even this is enough for God, not because we are good enough, but because God is good enough.

Another peculiar similarity between the woman and Jairus is that Jesus seemed to be playing a very passive role, at least in the beginning, for both individuals when they reached out to him. When Jairus first approached Jesus, Jesus simply seemed to go with the flow. Mark wrote, "So Jesus went with him" (5:24). It was almost like an automatic response, no questions asked. Jesus also seemed to allow the woman's plan to approach him to go fairly smoothly. No one noticed her or stopped her until she had been healed.

God does not stop us from approaching Him and seeking His help in our own ways. He knows and understands all human limitations. However, He will always show us who is really in charge by doing the unexpected and adjusting our perspective and experience of His power. God loves bringing out the contrasts between human impossibilities and God's possibilities.

So, although Jesus seemed to be passively 'going through the motions' in the first half of the story, when he asked the question, "Who touched my clothes?", he suddenly became a little too assertive and inflexible. He paused on his way to his house call just to seek the woman out among the crowd in broad daylight, exactly the opposite of what she had planned. This is when God's plan overrides human plans.

Was Jesus' question really necessary? Couldn't Jesus just stop the woman's bleeding and let her get on with life? Or perhaps he could have visited her home another day? Didn't Jesus know her medical condition was meant to be confidential? Wasn't Jesus aware that Jairus was about to have a heart attack? There was no time for Jesus to stick around in the crowd and wait for the woman to come out.

Jesus paused his rescue mission to save the reputable Jairus' daughter, in order to carry out another rescue mission to save a social outcast. Of course, he could do that because he had all the time in the world, and he had to seek this woman out! That was what Jesus did, no matter how much time it would take. "*Who touched my clothes?*" Jesus asked. Even the disciples thought the question was redundant and strange.

Have you ever been overwhelmed by the desperation and needs of the people surrounding you? Our world is full of people who are suffering and feeling despair, but even if we have the desire and compassion to help, we're defeated by all kinds of human limitations. We're limited in time, love, resources, strength, patience... The list of our inadequacies goes on. We are as trapped as the people we want to help, without the physical or mental capacity to seek out people in need, let alone save them from their distress. Sometimes the people we try to help in turn hurt us by passing on their sense of shame and burden onto us.

Yet for Jesus, his priorities are always different from ours. He is the only one who is able. While the woman saw it as an opportunity to be healed physically, Jesus wouldn't let go of this opportunity to completely restore a lost soul. Salvation is not about sneaking up to God, getting the bit of help we want, and then getting on with our lives. It means taking on a totally new identity and being born again. And God can do it.

What would you do if you were the woman? Would you come out and tell the whole world your story and reveal your uncleanliness?

By asking "Who touched my clothes?", Jesus was not shaming her in public, because he had already healed her bleeding. The shame had gone. By calling her out, Jesus had actually exposed to the whole crowd that he had been made unclean by an unclean woman. This would be terribly embarrassing and shameful for a respected religious leader. It could do unspeakable damage to his reputation as a rabbi. This would be the tabloid newspapers' favourite headline story!

Yet Jesus didn't mind that he was made 'unclean' by the woman. In fact, it was Jesus himself who took the initiative to show the world he had been touched by an unclean woman. To take up our uncleanliness was the key part of Jesus' mission on earth, and his willingness to do so is humanity's only hope.

Not only that, by calling her out, Jesus gave her a chance to wipe away all the shame and darkness in her past, while reinstating her dignity and giving her a new identity in front of the whole world. Jesus was there to create a window of opportunity to say to her, "Daughter, your faith has healed you. Go in peace and be freed from your suffering" (5:34). Jesus did all that so that he could call her 'daughter' in front of the whole world. This woman now had a home, beloved and restored—not only physically and emotionally, not only socially and culturally, but eternally with a new relationship with the Father in Heaven. No doctor or religious cleansing ritual could ever restore her to be the woman God had created her to be. An unwanted, unclean woman had now become a daughter of God. This was what she truly needed from Jesus.

Do we know what we truly need from Jesus?

7.

Why are you thinking these things in your hearts?

(Luke 5:17-26)

Palestine 30 A.D.

One day, you decide to go and check out this Jesus figure everyone in town is talking about. You find yourself in a house packed with people who have come to hear Jesus' teaching, including some of the prominent religious leaders you know. You can even smell the human sweat in the stuffy room. The atmosphere seems tense however, as you are surrounded by the Pharisees who are ready to pounce on Jesus at any time. This is not surprising, as Jesus' teachings about himself and how God's Kingdom works have already offended these leaders on many occasions.

While Jesus keeps talking, you can sense the tension escalating. Suddenly, there is a strange noise coming from above the house. Heads and eyes start to look up. Someone must be doing some work on the roof, you think. The noise gets louder and louder, until it becomes clear that whoever is on the roof is trying to break it open!

A commotion spreads across the crowd. The roof has opened!

"Ooooooh!" people exclaim, as a mat with a man lying on it is slowly being lowered through the hole in the roof by some men. The mat lands right in front of where Jesus is standing.

The man's body doesn't move at all. You recognize him as one of the paralyzed men in town. The religious leaders, however, are not too concerned about the paralyzed man's needs, nor are they worried about who would repair the roof. Their only concern is what they have come to check out: Jesus' power and authority, an issue of paramount significance indeed.

In fact, Jesus is just about to address the exact things they are thinking about in their hearts.

Let's read Luke 5:17-26.

> **17** One day Jesus was teaching, and Pharisees and teachers of the law were sitting there. They had come from every village of Galilee and from Judea and Jerusalem. And the power of the Lord was with Jesus to heal the sick. **18** Some men came carrying a paralyzed man on a mat and tried to take him into the house to lay him before Jesus. **19** When they could not find a way to do this because of the crowd, they went up on the roof and lowered him on his mat through the tiles into the middle of the crowd, right in front of Jesus. **20** When Jesus saw their faith, he said, "Friend, your sins are forgiven." **21** The Pharisees and the teachers of the law began thinking to themselves, "Who is this fellow who speaks

blasphemy? Who can forgive sins but God alone?"
22 Jesus knew what they were thinking and asked, "Why are you thinking these things in your hearts?

23 Which is easier: to say, 'Your sins are forgiven,' or to say, 'Get up and walk'?

24 But I want you to know that the Son of Man has authority on earth to forgive sins." So he said to the paralyzed man, "I tell you, get up, take your mat and go home." **25** Immediately he stood up in front of them, took what he had been lying on and went home praising God. **26** Everyone was amazed and gave praise to God. They were filled with awe and said, "We have seen remarkable things today."

Why do you think the paralyzed man's friends went to so much trouble to break through the roof, disrupt Jesus' talk, and risk all the awkwardness and embarrassment in front of the religious leaders? You're probably thinking, *they did this because they wanted Jesus to heal the man*, aren't you? Let's forget all the children's Sunday School answers and assumptions we've been brought up with. Actually, Scripture doesn't tell us why. We can only guess. It could be possible that they were eager to hear Jesus' teaching? Perhaps they wanted their sins forgiven, which would explain Jesus' response in verse 20? Or maybe they just wanted to get Jesus' autograph? We simply don't know.

No matter what their intentions were, we know one thing for sure: the man did not have an easy life. Being paralyzed is a tremendously difficult experience, and we can only imagine how much worse this would be in the first century. This man was unable to move his body for the rest of his life. That was a very desperate situation indeed. He must have been fully aware of how much he needed his friends' help in every part of his life. He couldn't even go near Jesus without his friends' dramatic act of opening someone else's roof.

And why did his friends need to break in through someone else's roof? Couldn't they have waited until Jesus had come outside again, or made an appointment to meet Jesus another time? The action on the roof not only highlighted the desperation and distress of the man in need, it also reflects the physical, social, emotional, as well as spiritual obstacles his friends had to go through in order to come before Jesus.

Bringing your needs and desperation to Jesus is never easy. We also face overwhelming difficulties physically, emotionally, socially, and spiritually. Perhaps your needs and obstacles are very different from those experienced by this paralyzed man, but we all need to recognise our needs, to have the same faith in Jesus, and to have the same perseverance in overcoming multitudes of hurdles to present ourselves in front of Jesus.

What is your most desperate need? Here is one question you can consider: what is in your mind when you wake up every morning? What pops up first in your head every day is what is affecting you the most, and that is what you need to bring to Jesus. Pay attention to your first thoughts every morning, lay them down on a mat, and lower it at Jesus' feet, just as the paralyzed man's friends did. We all need to do this day after day.

Luke's account doesn't tell us if these friends had said anything to Jesus, but we do know Jesus' response. In verse 20, Jesus said, "Friend, your sins are forgiven."

Wasn't that the most wonderful response anyone could get from Jesus? Well, apparently not for the Pharisees and teachers of the law who were there. They were furious! There was no hint of celebration in the text. No one seemed to care how the paralyzed man was feeling. No one asked about the roof or the poor owner of the house. These religious leaders only had one thing on their mind: Jesus had overstepped the limits of the authority they believed he should have. What Jesus said should have been something to celebrate about, but Jesus forgiving people's sins was a step too far for these self-righteous leaders to accept. They knew very clearly that only God has the authority to forgive sins. Here, Jesus publicly claimed to have this authority which was exclusive to God alone.

Then Jesus asked the Pharisees two awkward questions (verses 22-23), "Why are you thinking these things in your hearts? Which is easier: to say, 'Your sins are forgiven,' or to say, 'Get up and walk'?"

Do you think Jesus has the authority to forgive sins and to heal? Here, Jesus was not only talking about the 'ability' to do these things. What's the difference between 'authority' and 'ability'? In human terms, we know certain government officials or people in law enforcement have the authority to perform certain tasks in our society, though not necessarily the ability to do so!

Likewise, we might have the ability to do certain things, but it doesn't necessarily mean we have the authority over other people to do so. Authority is all about the person's identity and position in relation to others. The religious leaders imposed their own desired boundaries for Jesus' identity and position. This was what they were thinking in their hearts.

Does Jesus have the authority to cancel our debt of sins? Does he have the authority to heal us? Healing is not just about curing a disease. It implies transforming the darkest, most dysfunctional parts of our lives. The Pharisees knew this was the most fundamental question they had to address. And this question was as relevant to them as it is to us today. Do we also see the serious implications of this question in every aspect of our lives?

Jesus claims to have the authority to do both in our lives. He asked the people accusing him of blasphemy, "Which is easier: to say, 'Your sins are forgiven,' or to say, 'Get up and walk'?" Actually, for someone with total authority to do both, this question is irrelevant. These two commands would be equally easy and straightforward for Jesus, because he is the one in charge of both these realms of our lives.

The only question remaining is, do we really recognize Jesus' authority? And if so, what are we doing about it? Or do we want to set the boundaries to limit Jesus' authority over our lives? The paralyzed man and his friends not only recognized it (verse 20 tells us "Jesus saw their faith"), they also took action in the face of all the physical and social challenges in order to bring their desperate situation to Jesus, exposing themselves to public judgement and social ridicule. Jesus was worth all the trouble.

What obstacles do we have? Sometimes, we Christians subconsciously picture God as a harsh coach who pushes us to keep doing better or make a greater effort to improve ourselves to please Him. Actually, Scripture never gives us this picture. God wants to see a broken heart humbled by the painful awareness of our helplessness and desperation to be near Him.

At other times, we assume God simply demands us to have bigger faith. Well, that's not exactly what Scripture says either. In Jesus' teaching of the Parable of the Mustard Seed, during the healing of a demon-possessed boy (Matthew 17), we can see that Jesus isn't most concerned about how great our faith is, but the object of our faith. The father in the story also had pretty much no faith, but in the end, he was very honest about his lack of faith and asked Jesus for help. The object of his faith was correct, and that was what counted.

If it's not about the size of our faith, then what is it about? It's all about whom you have faith in. There is no point in having great faith in the wrong god. But when you recognize Jesus' authority in your life, even if you only have a little or even close to zero faith in Jesus, that's still okay with Jesus because it's all about him, not us. If we're relying on how great our faith is, we're still relying on ourselves. When our object of faith is correct, we can have perseverance even when the journey is full of all sorts of obstacles, because Jesus is bigger than all those problems combined. Ask Jesus for help with your unbelief.

What are your most desperate needs today? What hinders us from bringing them to Jesus? Yes, bring them to Jesus and trust him. He has the authority and the power.

8.

Where can we buy bread for these people to eat?

(John 6:1-15)

Bill is a well-known Christian chef in Hong Kong who integrates his faith into his cuisine. I once had the privilege to be invited to a wonderful Chinese restaurant he owns. All the food was amazing and various dishes on the menu had biblical references and names. One of these dishes was called "Five Loaves and Two Fish," named after one of the very few miracles recorded in all four Gospels.

The dish had, as you might have guessed, two large fish around the plate and five buns at the centre, but surrounding the fish and buns, there were also twelve small "baskets" created from orange skins and tomatoes stuffed with lots of other surprises inside. We were already quite full after eating the fish and buns, but we were still excited to dig into the twelve baskets to discover all the extra yummy delicacies hidden inside. Needless to say, we were filled to the brim with the wonderful food at the end. It was a feast of abundance.

The miracle of Jesus feeding five thousand people was a miraculous transformation from inadequacy to abundance. Yet, in reality, life is more often than not nowhere near the experience of abundance that diners can enjoy while eating

"Five Loaves and Two Fish" at Bill's restaurant. Inadequacy is something many of us Christians feel when we look at ourselves and our walk with God. We feel we are simply 'not good enough' in many things, especially when we reflect upon our calling. No matter how hard we try, we know deep in our hearts that we are never good enough. This is why I want to focus on a story about "spiritual increment" in Jesus.

Although the miracle is recorded in all four Gospels, John's narrative is unique. Let's dive into the text, John 6:1-15, and see what we notice:

> **1** Some time after this, Jesus crossed to the far shore of the Sea of Galilee (that is, the Sea of Tiberias), **2** and a great crowd of people followed him because they saw the signs he had performed by healing the sick. **3** Then Jesus went up on a mountainside and sat down with his disciples. **4** The Jewish Passover Festival was near. **5** When Jesus looked up and saw a great crowd coming toward him, he said to Philip, "Where shall we buy bread for these people to eat?" **6** He asked this only to test him, for he already had in mind what he was going to do. 7 Philip answered him, "It would take more than half a year's wages to buy enough bread for each one to have a bite!" **8** Another of his disciples, Andrew, Simon Peter's brother, spoke up, **9** "Here is a boy with five small barley loaves and two small fish, but how far will they go among so many?" **10** Jesus said, "Have the people sit down." There was plenty of grass in that place, and they sat down (about five thousand men

were there). **11** Jesus then took the loaves, gave thanks, and distributed to those who were seated as much as they wanted. He did the same with the fish. **12** When they had all had enough to eat, he said to his disciples, "Gather the pieces that are left over. Let nothing be wasted." **13** So they gathered them and filled twelve baskets with the pieces of the five barley loaves left over by those who had eaten. **14** After the people saw the sign Jesus performed, they began to say, "Surely this is the Prophet who is to come into the world." **15** Jesus, knowing that they intended to come and make him king by force, withdrew again to a mountain by himself.

Did you notice how many numbers there are in the story? 200, 5, 2, 5000, 12... Why do you think John included these numbers? Actually, Jesus didn't mention any of these numbers. They all came from his disciples or the people surrounding him, thus exposing their perspectives and mental calculations of what was happening. As humans, we love working out all the mathematics whenever we encounter a problem, especially when it involves money. John's narratives continuously highlight the problem of inadequate resources, as well as the question of where exactly they should come from. This was a very practical question because the math simply didn't add up!

Apart from the numbers, John also puts emphasis on the verb "to know" in order to highlight the fact that Jesus already knew what was going on. In verse 6, after Jesus asked Philip where they could find bread to feed all the people, John tells us that Jesus only asked Philip this so as to test him, because he already had in mind what he would do.

And in verse 15, John again emphasized that Jesus already knew:

> **15** Jesus, knowing that they intended to come and make him king by force, withdrew again to a mountain by himself.

So the beginning (verses 1-4) and the end (verses 14-15) of the story mirror each other nicely in highlighting Jesus' insights and knowledge. Jesus knew two important things. First, he knew about the people's true intentions for coming to see him, something that is exclusive to John's narrative. In verse 2, we are told that the crowd followed Jesus mainly because they saw the signs he had performed by healing the sick (verse 2). It was Passover at the time, a weekend of a heightened sense of nationalism, as the Jews were eagerly anticipating the arrival of their Messiah who would liberate them from the Romans' control. They came to witness Jesus perform more signs to check out if he would be the one to lead them to the political freedom they had been dreaming of.

Verse 14 also echoes this idea. When the people saw the miracle, they began to say, "Surely, this is the Prophet who is to come into the world." Who was "the Prophet" and what stirred up such anticipation among the people? The people's excitement was actually inspired by one of Moses' final instructions to the Israelites before his death, when he said,

"The Lord your God will raise up for you a prophet like me from among you, from your fellow Israelites" (Deuteronomy 18:15).

What would "a prophet like me (Moses)" look like? Under Moses' leadership, God rained down manna from heaven when the people did not have enough to eat, and led the whole nation out of slavery in Egypt in dramatic and triumphant ways. So the crowd came to Jesus during this "Independence Day" to check out if this former glorious liberation would happen again, allowing them to get rid of the Romans once and for all.

To put it more bluntly, the people were basically contemplating the possibility of a rebellion. A crowd of five thousand men would have been completely capable of starting a riot or even organizing a revolution against the Roman authorities. Therefore, any miraculous sign performed by Jesus that weekend could easily carry unintended political implications, and Jesus was fully aware of this from the beginning.

The second insight Jesus had concerned what to do about the situation. Jesus knew what the people truly needed, which was neither to be fed nor to overthrow the Romans, but to know God. Today, God has these same insights in every aspect of our lives. He knows all about our hidden agendas, as well as how to fulfil our deepest needs.

The same is true in our church ministries and in how we serve the people in our communities. God already knows everything happening in the most hidden corners of our hearts and minds, even when we go about our ministries. We may come to church with all sorts of intentions, but God has known us all even from before we were born, and He knows not only our deepest needs, but also the best way to provide for them—and that is one of the key messages of the Gospel.

In verses 5-9, Jesus took the initiative to ask the disciples a very difficult question, and John even tells us it was directed at Philip specifically: "Where shall we find bread for the people to eat?"

This was a momentous and scary task! Five thousand men plus their families! Jesus could have easily dismissed the crowd, arranged another date for the next event, and allowed the people to go home and eat. But instead, he asked the question because he *wanted* to feed the people and he wanted the disciples to be part of God's work.

We know the incident must have taken place in a large space outdoors, possibly in the semi-arid desert, to be able to hold more than five thousand men and their families. Providing food for thousands of people in the wilderness, totally impromptu, would be a momentous task. But Jesus insisted on feeding them and providing for their immediate physical needs, even when he was aware of their misconception of who he was. Yet, for the disciples, it was an important test as well as a lesson. How much did they really know their teacher and understand the heart of God? God always knows what to do about the colossal needs in our lives, but he also wants *us* to know what to do—to look to Him for provision.

So Jesus asked Philip, "Where shall we find bread for the people to eat?". Why do you think Jesus picked on Philip? The Gospel of Luke gives us a possible clue. The story took place around the city of Bethsaida, Philip's hometown. So Philip was a local. He grew up there. Bethsaida was *his* territory! When you need recommendations for the best bakeries and catering services in town, who else would be the best people to ask other than the locals?

However, the question was a tricky one for Philip because what could he say? Being in his own territory still didn't mean he had the ability to provide for the needs of the people. Jesus' question was a practical and yet puzzling one. Philip immediately activated his logical brain to work out the maths to answer Jesus' question. He could perhaps make a call to all the bakeries he knew in town? But even if every person only took one small bite, Philip thought, it would still cost two hundred denarii (approximately 8 months' worth of an average salary at the time). So even Philip's most conservative estimate was overwhelmingly unfeasible according to human economics. The needs were simply too great to meet.

While Philip measured the needs and costs, Andrew was assessing the resources available. In verse 9, Andrew spoke up, "Here is a boy with five small barley loaves and two small fish, but how far will they go among so many?"

I always find it interesting how John's Gospel often includes details that cannot be found in the other three Gospels. This time, John even tells us that the loaves were made of barley, an interesting reference to God's miraculous provision of barley loaves to Elisha to feed a hundred men (2 Kings 4:42-44).

Andrew's practical question perfectly echoed Philip's financial assessment: "How far will they go among so many?". Andrew wasn't seeking a mathematical answer, but his question was an expression of his panic and sense of despair. Both disciples could only see the glaring inadequacy of what they had to provide for the needs of the people.

This was pure irony. The crowd came to see Jesus with the excited anticipation of seeing him perform miracles and signs (although with the wrong intentions). Yet the disciples' attitudes posed a staggering contrast in their expectations, or the lack thereof. Expecting Jesus to perform a miracle seemed to be the last thing on their minds. How ironic and sad is that? Those who were following Jesus most closely were the ones expecting the least from him.

Let's look at the resources available. Have you ever wondered why a child would carry five barley loaves and two fish with him? We can reasonably speculate his situation: he probably came as part of a family of five and the food was meant to be the dinner for the family. If you were a parent who came to the event well-prepared, would you eagerly volunteer your family's dinner to a crowd of five thousand strangers while some anxious disciples went around asking for food? Most likely not. I can imagine the grown-ups of the family nervously trying to keep quiet and unnoticed, while the innocent child was waving his hand excitedly because he had something to show to Jesus. His innocence meant that he couldn't see the inadequacy of what he had to offer from a human perspective.

In God's economy, resources are not to be measured or worked out but surrendered. Note Jesus used the word "where", not "how". "*Where* shall we find bread for the people to eat?" The question was essentially a reminder of where our true resources come from. Where shall we find enough resources for the needs of the world? Resources from ourselves are never enough, but resources from God are always in abundance. When we admit our resources are inadequate, then we can look up to God and rely solely on His resources.

Jesus answered Andrew's question by doing three things. First, he told the disciples to instruct the crowd to take a seat on the grass. The act of sitting down usually comes with an attitude of anticipation; it means to relax and get ready to enjoy something. John's description of the event specifically mentions there was plenty of grass in that place for people to sit down on (verse 10). Was it a coincidence that a piece of grassland was available on that day, large enough for five thousand plus families to sit down on and comfortably enjoy a picnic together? God even had this prepared. One can imagine the tremendous difference a piece of comfortable grassland would have made for the thousands of weary people on that day.

The picture reminds us of the compassion of Jesus the Bible specifically depicts. When Jesus saw the people were like sheep without a shepherd, he was full of compassion for them (Matthew 9:36). What a beautiful pictorial reference to the opening of the famous Psalm 23, "The Lord is my shepherd, I shall not want. He makes me lie down in green pastures."

The beginning of John's narrative tells us it was originally a private meeting between Jesus and the disciples (verse 1), meaning there would be a maximum of thirteen people. It was only when Jesus looked up and saw a big crowd of people approaching him (verse 2) that the meeting suddenly turned into one large party. Yet even with the venue, God had already prepared and provided in such minute detail for what people would need on that day. Have we ever considered that the places, circumstances, and resources which we encounter each day are all provided by God for us to partner with Him in His work?

The second thing Jesus did was to give thanks and to distribute the food. There were no sophisticated, jaw-dropping performances, only a simple ordinary act of handing out food to a hungry crowd. God can do miracles through ordinary people in ordinary ways. John also highlighted that the distribution allowed people to get "as much as (they) wanted" (verse 11). Jesus was not giving out stingy 'communion-sized' bites. Jesus did not say to crowd, "Everyone, please be considerate and take a small portion first. We will arrange the second helping after everyone has had some food." No, it wasn't like that at all. It was an all-you-can-eat feast. God's provision is always unlimited for us. It's usually our lack of faith and imagination that limit God, to the point where we often nullify God's power.

The third action Jesus instructed was to gather the leftovers. Here John gives us another specific number in his account: twelve baskets of leftovers! Why did Jesus want the leftovers collected? Understandably, he didn't want the food to be wasted, but it must have been a shocking experience for the disciples. What do you think was going through their minds while they were collecting the leftovers? Just not long ago, they were overwhelmed by their anxiety based on their perceived impossibility of meeting the needs of the people. Little did they know that they would have too much rather than too little. God is a God of surprising abundance.

Have you ever had the experience of gathering "leftovers" of God's goodness? In our church ministries, we have witnessed how God has done amazing work among individuals and families who have needs far greater than the church could ever meet. Sometimes we don't even realize how little resources we have. But with God's help, and only with God's help, we can serve the community.

Hudson Taylor, a British missionary to China in the late nineteenth century, was the founder of the China Inland Mission (now OMF International). The mission had always served purely by faith, relying solely on God's provision without any kind of fundraising. In his diary, he wrote:

> "Our Father is a very experienced One. He knows very well that His children wake up with a good appetite every morning, and He always provides breakfast for them, and does not send them supperless to bed at night. 'Thy bread shall be given thee, and thy water shall be sure.' He sustained three million Israelites in the wilderness for forty years. We do not expect He will send three million missionaries to China, but if He did, He would have ample means to sustain them all. Let us see that we keep God before our eyes; that we walk in His ways and seek to please and glorify Him in everything, great and small. Depend upon it, God's work done in God's way will never lack God's supplies."

Sometimes we worry whether God's provision will be adequate for us. Instead, on the contrary, we should be concerned whether our lack of faith and understanding might limit God's miracles. God's provisions are always ample for our needs, and He has already prepared them. It would be a tragic waste if we still can't learn this lesson.

Like in the story, sometimes our private meeting with Jesus can unexpectedly be turned into a mega-feast of God's goodness and power. But where can we find the resources to meet the needs of all the people around us? In Jesus, the Bread of Life, you can. Yes, you can welcome more people to enjoy God's feast with you than you ever thought. Yes, you can distribute the resources prepared by God to the people God has called you to serve, and yes, remember not to waste the leftovers!

9.

Has no one condemned you?

(John 8:1-11)

Whilst I was standing in a church service worshipping and partaking in the Lord's Supper, I was suddenly touched by an overwhelming realization: If it were not for Jesus, who chose to show mercy to us and willingly stood in the position of sinners like us, taking our place, we would never have had the Gospel of the cross in human history. The Gospel is all about Jesus giving up his position and taking ours.

Today I'd like to share a story about 'positions'. In fact, the Bible has a lot to say about being in the right 'positions'.

I know of a couple who turned to marriage counselling for help with their constant state of arguing. The counsellor encouraged them to switch positions, stand in each other's shoes, and simply look at things from each other's viewpoint. They reluctantly agreed, and as they tried, they gradually began to understand each other's situation and feelings more. Then the counsellor asked them to return to their own positions and see how things had become different. The couple were shocked to discover something totally new about themselves, and how a lot of their issues, reactions, and personality traits were in fact deeply rooted in their childhood experiences involving their own parents. The counsellor then suggested that they imagine themselves as children, face their parents again as children, and reconsider how their previous experience had affected their present selves. As a result, their marriage improved dramatically through this journey of healing and discovery.

Our positions and viewpoints are the most fundamental factors affecting how we perceive and experience everything in life. The positions we take determine what we see, and our reactions will vary accordingly.

However, there is one position we should never be in: the position of the Creator. We can never be God. Yet, ironically, it is the position many of us are too eager to take, because it gives us a self-righteous licence to judge other people's flaws and impose our values on everything in life. We Christians are no better. Consciously or subconsciously, we may consider ourselves wiser and more superior. Not only do we constantly judge each other in the church, we also love criticizing those outside as well.

There are two passages in the Bible, one in the New Testament and one in the Old, that deal with the 'positions' we take. On the surface, they are totally unrelated to each other and to us in the twentieth century, but they are in fact very much interrelated and relevant to us. Let's look at the New Testament passage first in John 8: 1-8.

> **1** But Jesus went to the Mount of Olives. **2** At dawn he appeared again in the temple courts, where all the people gathered around him, and he sat down to teach them. **3** The teachers of the law and the Pharisees brought in a woman caught in adultery. They made her stand before the group **4** and said

to Jesus, "Teacher, this woman was caught in the act of adultery. **5** In the Law Moses commanded us to stone such women. Now what do you say?" **6** They were using this question as a trap, in order to have a basis for accusing him. But Jesus bent down and started to write on the ground with his finger. **7** When they kept on questioning him, he straightened up and said to them, "Let any one of you who is without sin be the first to throw a stone at her." **8** Again he stooped down and wrote on the ground.

Why did people suddenly bring a woman caught in adultery to Jesus? John tells us their intention very clearly: to lay a trap to test Jesus. As written in the Torah in the Old Testament, an adulterous woman should be stoned to death. Adultery was one of the sins punishable by death in the Law of Moses. It was written in a black-and-white manner in the Torah. But why was this a trap for Jesus? The problem was that at that time, the Jews were under the rule of the Roman Empire, whose laws stated that Jews were not allowed to execute the death penalty by themselves.

In other words, this was a golden opportunity for anyone who wanted to trap Jesus by creating a public scandal. The question forced Jesus to choose a stance in a tricky political and religious dilemma to show if he was more loyal to the Law of Moses by executing the death penalty, or more loyal to the Romans by not executing the woman. Either option could lead to great trouble for Jesus, or so they thought.

How should Jesus respond to this problem? From which angle should he judge? Should he obey the Old Testament law as a respected Jewish Rabbi, or the Roman authorities as a law-abiding citizen? The religious leaders had apparently come up with a foolproof scheme against Jesus.

As noted, the trap was all about choosing the right stance. Jesus' immediate response was rather strange. Instead of giving a sermon on the Kingdom of God, Jesus said nothing and just "bent down and started to write on the ground with his finger" (John 8:6). Was he stunned by the situation and trying to avoid saying anything? Was he fiddling his fingers on the ground just to buy more time to think of a good answer? Verse 8 repeats the same action, "So he bent down again and used his finger to draw on the ground." What on earth was Jesus doing? Scripture only gives us a very simple description of Jesus writing on the ground, but not what he was writing.

Suspense. We all want to know what exactly Jesus was writing. If Scripture tells us Jesus did it twice, then it is probably something important, right? On the surface, Jesus seemed rather passive and hesitant, but for the those who were familiar with the Old Testament, Jesus' repeated act of writing with his finger might ring a bell. Where in the Old Testament can you find a story of someone "writing with the finger" and doing it twice? Those who sought to trick Jesus using the Law of Moses would certainly know the answer. This story would give us important clues to help us better understand Jesus' message. So let us see how Jesus actually answered the people's question and how he actively chose his stance.

In Exodus 31, God had led the Israelites out of slavery in Egypt through many amazing miracles and wonders. As they approached Mount Sinai, God made a covenant with the Israelites, but God only called Moses to go up the mountain because the people couldn't approach God due to their sins. God spoke to Moses, then wrote the law on stone tablets and gave them to him. How was the law written? Not by Moses, but by God himself, "with his fingers". The tablets of stone were inscribed by the finger of God (Exodus 31:18).

Yet why did God do it twice? Chapter 32 unfolds the events for us. When Moses brought the stone tablets down the mountain, he witnessed a despicable scene. The Israelites had convinced Aaron, their priest, to cast a golden calf for them to worship! They committed idolatry, while God was establishing a covenant of love and mercy with them! Just like the woman who had been caught while committing adultery (John 8:4), they were caught red-handed.

Moses was so angry that he threw the stone tablets to the ground right on the spot and broke them (Exodus 32:19). But God never gave up on His people, despite their repeated betrayals and rebellion against Him. He told Moses, "Chisel out two stone tablets like the first ones, and I will write on them the words that were on the first tablets, which you broke. Be ready in the morning, and then come up on Mount Sinai. Present yourself to me there on top of the mountain" (Exodus 34:1-2). So God Himself continued to extend His covenant with His people and wrote the law the second time.

When Jesus used his finger to write on the ground, the Jews present who claimed to know Moses' Law should have been able to recognize Jesus' gestures as a clear reference to the story on Mount Sinai. The plots were painfully familiar and similar. Both involved a serious sin punishable by death, sandwiched between two acts of writing with a finger. But what exactly was Jesus trying to say?

The Jewish leaders proudly saw themselves in the same position as Moses was in, because they were the ones who caught this woman red-handed while she was committing adultery, just as Moses caught the Israelites worshipping the golden calf. They immediately arrested her and brought her before Jesus to test how far he would also 'obey' Moses' Law like they did. Yet Jesus' act of writing on the ground with his finger showed that he was not standing in Moses' position to enforce the law—he was writing as God himself, the one who wrote the Law with his finger.

Jesus' unexpected act posed a direct challenge to everyone present to immediately rethink their true position, Jesus' position, as well as the position of the woman, in the whole scenario.

What was the woman's position? John 8:3 specifically describes the position where the woman was standing in a rather peculiar way: "The teachers of the law and the Pharisees brought in a woman caught in adultery. They made her stand before the group (in the midst of them)."

The Greek expression "standing in the midst" is emphasized twice in John's original narrative, though not clearly highlighted in many of our modern translations. Mentioning this twice is significant indeed. In addition to verse 3, we see the same expression in verse 9 as John describes the people's reaction to Jesus' surprising statement: "At this, those who heard began to go away one at a time, the older ones first, until only Jesus was left, with the woman still *standing in the midst.*" So John particularly highlights the position of this woman as "standing in the midst." What's the point of this?

Let's return to the story on Mount Sinai in Exodus. God was the one who made the Law and He gave it through Moses. God clearly stated that no one could go up to Mount Sinai because His holiness would mean that anyone who went up would surely die. None of the people could approach God; only Moses could. So everyone else had to stay and wait at the bottom of Mount Sinai.

When Moses went up to Mount Sinai, what position was he standing in? In Exodus 34:2, we know God instructed Moses to go up the mountain once again after the incident of the golden calf. Later, verse 5 tells us that God "came down in the cloud and stood there with him and proclaimed His name, the Lord." The passage specifically mentions twice that Moses went up to Mount Sinai to wait for God, and the author of Exodus clearly describes Moses as "standing in the midst" while meeting God.

Indeed, the religious people in John's story were more than happy to take Moses' position to judge the woman and coerce Jesus into taking the same position to condemn her to death. However, according to the text, who was in Moses' position now? It was the woman herself! She was the one "standing in the midst", just as Moses had stood on Mount Sinai ready to receive the law before God.

Where did the Jews and Pharisees stand then? Jesus said to them, "Whoever among you is without sin can take a stone and throw at her first." As a result, no one dared do anything.

In mirroring the incident at Mount Sinai, these people were actually standing in the same position as the Israelites were thousands of years before.

As no one was good enough to go up to Mount Sinai to see God, similarly, no one—not even the most pious of religious leaders—was qualified to throw stones at this woman. The only one standing in the midst was Moses, and now this woman. That was why Jesus asked the woman, "Has no one condemned you?" (John 8:10). Weren't there a lot of people condemning her just a few moments ago? No, no one was condemning her anymore.

In the story of the golden calf, only Moses was innocent. Even Aaron, the priest chosen by God, was actively involved in the idolatry and was caught red-handed together with the people! Moses was furious, understandably, but he chose not to condemn them. Exodus 32 tells us that, on the following day, Moses took the initiative to intercede for mercy and forgiveness on behalf of the people who had broken his heart (Exodus 32:11-14).

Moses was willing to stand in the midst of the Israelites, in the position of the sinners, and beg God for mercy. His strength and compassion were rooted in his understanding of God's nature:

> "The Lord, the Lord, the compassionate and gracious God, slow to anger, abounding in love and faithfulness, maintaining love to thousands, and forgiving wickedness, rebellion and sin. Yet he does not leave the guilty unpunished; he punishes the

children and their children for the sin of the parents to the third and fourth generation" (Exodus 34:6-7).

Just as Moses stood in the place of sinners and begged God for mercy on behalf of the Israelites committing adultery, Jesus also chose not to condemn the woman. Instead, he chose the cross, took the position of sinners, and took all the punishment and shame of the world upon himself.

Today, in the midst of all the sin and pain we have created in our society and in the church, do we stand in the position of a judge to condemn others while we are also sinners?

We know from the latter parts of Exodus that even Moses himself sinned against God and failed to enter the Promised Land. Even Moses himself had to stand in the midst to be judged. God's everlasting covenant with the Israelites was finally fulfilled in God sending His own Son. Our only hope is in God's mercy through the cross, not in throwing stones at each other. While we may enjoy fantasizing about standing in the position of God or Moses and judging the world, we are actually standing in the same position as the Israelites, and our only hope is in God's mercy alone.

How do we stop throwing stones at people?

A church fellowship group I know was once troubled by one of its female members who had all sorts of mental health issues and never had any breakthrough despite their best efforts to help. Yet when the lady finally opened up and shared horrific childhood experiences of abuse and trauma, her church friends finally understood where she was coming from. Their judgmental attitude towards her turned into compassion once they learned to see life in her shoes.

I had a classmate in medical school who used to be very judgemental of parents whose kids were covered with nasal mucus all over the face. We have all seen kids like that. He told me he would never allow his child to have such a filthy face. Later, this man got married and became a father. Guess what? He confessed to me, even as a doctor, he had given up on cleaning his child's face because his nose just kept running! Now he finally understood the people he had been judging because he found himself in their position, encountering the same situation.

Another woman I know confessed to me how she used to criticize mothers who would not keep an eye on their autistic children. There was a well-known case in the media about an autistic teenager who disappeared at the Hong Kong border while he was out with his familly. This woman thought the teenager's parents had failed miserably, until, as it happened, she also gave birth to a child with autism, and her perspective totally changed. Her son even went missing on numerous occasions! We learn not to throw stones when we find ourselves in the same position.

Christians love throwing stones too. When we listen to sermons, do we really open our hearts and listen to what God is saying? Or do we enjoy giving critiques as if we were sermon commentators? Some of us who have been Christians for a long time love to compare preachers or pick theological holes in the sermons we hear. I teach preaching in a Bible seminary; I have to keep reminding myself when I listen to my students' sermons that I am there to first listen to what God has to say to me rather than focus on giving a critique.

The passage also reminded me of a time when the media constantly reported about a local pastor who was convicted of sexual assault against a female member of his church. I kept hearing responses from other Christians, such as "I'm glad I'm not in that church", or "Oh, that would never happen in my denomination!" Really? Are we any better when we stand in front of our Creator if He is to judge us?

Before we judge anything or anyone, we must first look to God, then look at ourselves in relation to God, then we will know where we stand. Only then will we see that there is no difference between ourselves and whoever we are judging. Only then will we be able to see both ourselves and others through God's lens of holiness and mercy.

Compassion is not connivance. Acceptance does not equal approval. Jesus bluntly implied the woman had sinned. His question for the woman was not "Have you sinned?" But rather it was, "Has no one condemned you?", encouraging the woman to take a look at the accusers around her. Those who were condemning her realized they themselves were also sinners, and quickly and quietly made their exit. The Law of Moses stipulated that two or three witnesses must testify before a person could be put to death. So now, there were not enough witnesses to condemn her. In other words, Jesus was following the Law of Moses all along. The reality the religious leaders failed to see was that only Jesus was qualified to condemn her, but he chose to say, "I don't condemn you either. Go and sin no more" (John 8:11).

This is the stance God chose for the Israelites, for this woman, and for you and me. We are all standing in the midst of sinners as sinners, so we can never be judges. But we are standing under the mercy of God, who sent His Son in our midst to intercede for our forgiveness and bear our condemnation. Jesus had the authority to take the position of God, yet he willingly stood in the position of the sinners on the cross. Has no one condemned you? No, and with God's mercy we can face any sin, any weakness, and any struggle, as we learn to build each other up with Jesus' compassion. This is the Gospel in the story.

10.

How long should I put up with you?

(Mark 9:14-29)

During Sunday services, many of us worship with gusto. We pour our hearts into singing lyrics about putting all our trust in God no matter the circumstances. But do we honestly mean the words we sing? Do we trust God no matter what?

I have been feeling rather down recently. A few people I knew have committed suicide and passed away. These people included Christians—one of whom even came to our church—but they chose to end their lives prematurely in their own ways. Sadly, this phenomenon is becoming more and more common in our society today and becoming less and less shocking to us. I also noticed that these people I knew who ended their own lives didn't seem to be in any extreme or dire situation; they had simply lost their hope and the will to live.

When we find ourselves in a place where we feel utterly hopeless and helpless, where is our hope and help? Whenever we Christians deal with struggles in life, we say we can pray with faith, but what exactly does "praying with faith" mean? Apart from the Lord's Prayer, the Gospels have not given us many examples of Jesus teaching about this explicitly. Yet there are stories where Jesus' actions and dialogue can directly teach us about praying with faith.

Let's turn to an interesting story in Mark 9:14-29. Mark's narrative here is a classic example of chiasm in biblical literature. This means that the passage contains a symmetrical structure, with the first part being mirrored by the second part in a reversed order, and with the story's focal point sandwiched right in the middle. Here we see a structure of A-B-C-D-C-B-A:

A: v.14 - (The crowd discussing why the disciples had failed)

"When they came to the other disciples, they saw a large crowd around them and the teachers of the law arguing with them."

B: v.15 - (The crowd's reaction)

"As soon as all the people saw Jesus, they were overwhelmed with wonder and ran to greet him."

C: v.16-18 - (The father explaining his son's situation to Jesus)

"'What are you arguing with them about?" he asked. A man in the crowd answered, "Teacher, I brought you my son, who is possessed by a spirit that has robbed him of speech. 18 Whenever it seizes him, it throws him to the ground. He foams at the mouth, gnashes his teeth and becomes rigid. I asked your disciples to drive out the spirit, but they could not.'"

D: v.19-20 - (Jesus' question)

'"You unbelieving generation," Jesus replied, "how long shall I stay with you? How long shall I put up with you? Bring the boy to me."'

C: v.21-24 - (The father explaining his son's situation to Jesus and asking for help)

'Jesus asked the boy's father, "How long has he been like this?" "From childhood," he answered. "It has often thrown him into fire or water to kill him. But if you can do anything, take pity on us and help us." "'If you can'?" said Jesus. "Everything is possible for one who believes." Immediately the boy's father exclaimed, "I do believe; help me overcome my unbelief!"'

B: v.25-27 - (The crowd's reaction)

'When Jesus saw that a crowd was running to the scene, he rebuked the impure spirit. "You deaf and mute spirit," he said, "I command you, come out of him and never enter him again." The spirit shrieked, convulsed him violently and came out. The boy looked so much like a corpse that many said, "He's dead." But Jesus took him by the hand and lifted him to his feet, and he stood up.'

A: v.28-29 - (The disciples asked why they had failed)

'After Jesus had gone indoors, his disciples asked him privately, "Why couldn't we drive it out?" He replied, "This kind can come out only by prayer."'

The story tells of a boy possessed by demons and his helpless father trying to seek help from Jesus' disciples, but for some reason they all failed to make the demons leave the poor boy. Then Jesus arrived. The Master is here, what a relief! What would you do if you saw Jesus arrive? Well, of course, ask him for help! What else would you do?

Yet this was not what we see in Mark's narrative. There was neither excitement nor relief in the conversation when Jesus arrived at the scene. Whenever we read stories of Jesus healing the sick or casting out demons, we would expect to find somewhere in the beginning of the story either the people in need desperately coming to Jesus, or someone they know asking Jesus for help. However, in this text we cannot find any mention of this. The people ran to greet Jesus, but not to ask him for help.

The disciples were so occupied with discussing and debating amongst themselves that not one single person thought of bringing the child to Jesus. Even when Jesus was literally standing in front of them, no one seemed to have thought of it! The disciples had a lot of experience in exorcism, but they didn't do the most obvious thing they should do—bring the matter to Jesus.

Whenever we face difficulties and hardships in life, we usually resort to our technical know-how, or theories and solutions that we are proud of. We humans know how to do all sorts of things, except to pray and bring the matter to God. To the disciples, the boy was a problem to solve, or a situation to be analysed, or a topic to be discussed. Although there is nothing wrong with solving problems and analysing, what the disciples were doing was the opposite to praying. They tried to do it their way instead of confessing that their way was not working.

It turned out that Jesus was the one who had to ask the people present to explain the situation: "What are you arguing with them about?" Surely Jesus knew what was going on, but he had to ask the question just to be included in the conversation, because apparently no one had considered including him in the picture yet. Everyone was too busy arguing among themselves. The boy's father answered Jesus,

> **17** "Teacher, I brought you my son, who is possessed by a spirit that has robbed him of speech. **18** Whenever it seizes him, it throws him to the ground. He foams at the mouth, gnashes his teeth and becomes rigid. I asked your disciples to drive out the spirit, but they could not."

What do you notice about this father's reply? If we call this a 'prayer' (because he seemed to know who Jesus was and was talking to him), what do you think about this prayer? He described the situation and the problem to Jesus, as if Jesus didn't know anything, and then bluntly pointed out the people who failed to help. But something seemed missing in his prayer.

In the Gospels, we read about stories of parents with children in need coming to beg Jesus for help. We expect a line something like, "Teacher, please help my son." But no, this father said quite a lot to Jesus, but there was no asking for help!

He ended with, "I asked your disciples... but they could not." The end. There was not the slightest intention to try out Jesus, nor was there any hint of, "Jesus, what about you?"

Like many of us, the father was so overwhelmed with despondency that he didn't even know how to pray, and sadly the disciples simply aggravated his sense of despair by not only failing to cast out the demon from the boy, but also by failing to help the father to turn his attention to Jesus himself. According to the father, the problem lay with the disciples. If only they were able to do it, things would have been fine. Very often this is what hopelessness does to our mind. It's reassuring and comforting to have something or someone to blame, in order to justify our decision to leave God out of the picture. It means we don't need to turn to God for help. Finding a scapegoat is easier than seeking God. What we blame for our problem usually reveals what we truly believe in. What we blame is where we place our trust.

Jesus does not give up even when we have given up. He took the initiative to ask questions to guide this man to arrive at the point he needed to be in, in order to ask for help. But Jesus' response seemed harsh and strange,

> **19** "You unbelieving generation, how long shall I stay with you? How long shall I put up with you? Bring the boy to me."

That wasn't a very sympathetic and encouraging reply, was it? Was Jesus running out of patience?

One important thing we should take note of here is that Jesus didn't say that the father or the disciples were not praying enough or had too little faith, which is often what we think our problem is. Jesus was simply saying the real answer was to bring the boy to him, as he had said, "Let the little children come to me, and do not hinder them, for the kingdom of heaven belongs to such as these" (Matthew 19:14). Not bringing the boy to Jesus showed they were, as Jesus put it, "unbelieving" (i.e., they didn't believe at all). As far as Jesus was concerned, the problem was not that they had little faith, but that they had *zero* faith! Only when we bring matters to God can there be real hope. So how can God help us when we don't even bring our matters to Him?

Next, Jesus continued to ask questions to make the boy's father see the real problem. He asked, "How long has he been like this?" (verse 21). Jesus asked a rather strange question which he clearly knew the answer to; this was very typical of him, but it was a way to bring the helpless father from a point of disillusioned anguish to a breakthrough by pointing to the real origin of the problem. Now the father had to reflect on the root of the issue, which wasn't in the disciples.

The question of "How long?" is a profound one in all human problems. Tracing back to the beginning of our issues brings us to a place where we face what we must face. Very often the answer lies where the problem first began. In my ministries I have seen so many cases of depression, abuse, anxiety, and trauma, many being passed from one generation to another as part of the family pattern. A lot of traumatic cycles in families are totally out of human control. Even the best professional therapists in the world cannot deal with the powerful destructive forces in trauma. The only way out is simply to bring the matter to God. Only God can intervene and break the strongholds, because it is never about theories, theologies, or therapies. That was why the debates the disciples were engaged in were totally futile.

Jesus was guiding the father to go back to the origins of the issue in the boy. Notice this time, the father's answer was a little different. After answering Jesus' question, he added something extra, "But if you can do anything, take pity on us and help us" (verse 22).

For the first time, the father learned to turn his attention to Jesus himself. This was a turning point in his prayers. Prayer is confessing that you have failed and cannot do it yourself. The individuals I knew who committed suicide, including Christians, all had one thing in common: they tried to deal with their struggles by themselves, even to the point of death. They had the "hang in there" or the "yes I can do it" attitude that our modern society often celebrates, and when they finally realized they couldn't do it, that was when the shock of reality eventually made them turn to self-destruction.

The end of all hope for us is the beginning of hope in God. It is only when we reach the end of our road that we find there is another road we have been neglecting all along––He is our only way out. This was what the father finally realized: he was running out of options, and the only one left was to ask Jesus for help. I suspect even the disciples still didn't realize this point at that time. The disciples were still trying out different techniques, hoping eventually they would figure out one method that would work for this boy. They were still debating even after Jesus had come to them, not realizing that no human effort or knowledge could have saved the boy.

Christians have no problem in believing that God is our refuge, but do we know that He is our *only* refuge? Very often, seeing our absolute hopelessness is our only hope. This is the irony because that's the time when we can finally turn to God, our only source of hope in the first place, and pray. I'm not surprised that God sometimes allows us to drive ourselves into extremely desperate situations. I surely hope God doesn't need to do this to us to make us see how much we need Him! If only we knew from the start that God is our only way out, we could spare ourselves so much pain and suffering. Therefore, never try to deal with life with the "tough it out" or "suck it up" attitude. This might be what we are taught by the world, but it is not how God's creation works.

Now, let's see how the father prayed after this realization. In verse 22, he said to Jesus, "But if you can do anything, take pity on us and help us." Did he sound like he really believed in Jesus? This was not a very impressive prayer. The father sounded like he was simply testing the water. Perhaps he did not want to put too much hope in Jesus just in case it would lead to more disappointment, a pattern he probably had experienced?

Jesus' response was a significant one, "'If you can'? Everything is possible for one who believes" (verse 23). Unfortunately, many of our modern translations have failed to capture Jesus' meaning and tone accurately in the first part of Jesus' reply. These modern translations write, "If you can believe", which is not what the original Greek text means at all.

There was no "believe" in the first part of Jesus' reply. Jesus was simply repeating exactly what the father had said and reflecting it as a question back to him, "If you can?".

The father suddenly realized there was a faint ray of hope of finding a way out, and he wanted it. Next, he turned his attention to another fundamental issue: his own faith. He said another prayer that marked a second milestone in his very steep learning curve, "I do believe; help me with my unbelief!" (verse 24).

One very important thing we need to see in this father's prayer was that he was not asking for help for his insufficiency in faith, but for his unbelief—his state of not believing at all. The literal translation of the father's prayer was, "I believe. Help me with my unbelief." It wasn't a question of how much faith he had (a question Christians often focus on). Rather, he was saying that he did not believe at all!

What a self-contradicting statement! First, he said he believed, then immediately in the same sentence, he said he didn't believe. This is what the original text says. So then, did he believe or not?

In other words, he realized he did not have the faith in Jesus as he had wished. Actually, this father was making a very honest confession. Aren't we in the same situation? We want to believe in God in the midst of our struggles, but we ourselves are simply unable to believe. We human beings are this hopeless. We have the Bible that explains so many things about God directly to us, but can we believe it? No, when life gets tough, we realize we can't.

So the father's prayer wasn't a strange prayer after all, but a very authentic one. His own lack of faith was what he needed to come to terms with. Finally, after all these years, this father had arrived at the right place with God—he had to ask Jesus for help with his unbelief.

Some of us might wonder what we would do in such a conflicting situation. Shouldn't we try harder to 'squeeze' a little bit more faith out of ourselves first before approaching Jesus? We like to tell ourselves, "Let me have more faith first, *then* I'll go to God." No, because like this father, we aren't even able to do that. He was not even able to have faith, but he begged Jesus for help, and this was precisely where Jesus was trying to lead him to.

Was this 'unbelief' okay for Jesus? Was it acceptable to him? Yes! Jesus understood his state of unbelief and was more than willing to reach out to him. This is what the Good News is all about. God can help us even in our unbelief. Faith is a gift, so even faith itself depends on God, not on us. The moral of the story is, bring all your problems to God, *including* your unbelief. Just tell Him directly, "Help me with my unbelief!" Do not wait until you have some faith to pray, because we all need to ask God for help even in this first step of seeking His help. Both prayer and faith are about knowing you cannot "tough it out" on your own.

This is why a person who doesn't yet believe in God can also pray! Have you heard unbelieving seekers pray to God? Their prayers are never full of confidence or fancy Christian jargon, but something as blunt and as down-to-earth as, "God, I don't know if you're real, but if you are, show me". This is the kind of prayer God listens to—a sincere prayer that asks God to intervene in a helpless situation, even when the person is still living in unbelief. God meets us in our unbelief, not in our pretence of faith.

Jesus actively guided the father in his transition from a place of people-blaming to an honest prayer for help in his own unbelief. He also opened the disciples' eyes to the true meaning of prayer. Christians are often too busy working things out with their theology, ministry experiences, biblical knowledge, and all sorts of methods and strategies, as if these are what the Gospel is about. Prayer is not a 'tool' for us to utilize. It's a confession, a declaration of brokenness in our lives, "God, I can't do it. You come rescue me." Prayer is not about what the mouth is saying. It's an attitude. It's all about the hands. But I'm not saying you need to put your hands together while praying. I'm talking about letting go of whatever you have been holding onto and handing it over to God. Then you can open your empty hands to receive the grace God has prepared for you.

11.

Which one loves him more?

(Luke 7:36-50)

Hollywood movies are always about the "good guys" verses the "bad guys." Very often, our worldview is the same. If someone asked you to name a "good" public figure, worthy of your appreciation and respect, you might need to think for a while. But if you are asked to name a "bad" person, a few names might probably pop into your head fairly quickly.

Jesus had once found himself in the presence of both the "good" and the "bad" guys in the eyes of society, but for him, the question was not who's the good one and who isn't. He had different concerns: "Which one loves him more?". What an awkward question! What is even more puzzling is the way that Jesus kept connecting this question with the idea of debt.

Let's look at the opening of the story in Luke 7:36-40.

36 When one of the Pharisees invited Jesus to have dinner with him, he went to the Pharisee's house and reclined at the table. 37 A woman in that town who lived a sinful life learned that Jesus was eating at the Pharisee's house, so she came there with an alabaster jar of perfume. 38 As she stood behind him at his feet weeping, she began to wet his feet

with her tears. Then she wiped them with her hair, kissed them and poured perfume on them. **39** When the Pharisee who had invited him saw this, he said to himself, "If this man were a prophet, he would know who is touching him and what kind of woman she is—that she is a sinner." **40** Jesus answered him, "Simon, I have something to tell you." "Tell me, teacher," he said.

The Pharisees were the most pious followers of Judaism at the time, enjoying high social status and respect from the public. In this story, a Pharisee invited Jesus to eat at his house. Readers who are familiar with stories involving the Pharisees in the Bible would know this was a bit unusual. This Pharisee, unquestionably a "good" person in his social circle, probably admired Jesus or liked to listen to his preaching. No one in the story questioned his status or worthiness when he invited Jesus to eat with him in his house.

Then came the "bad" person. Luke's introduction of this woman seems to imply the whole town had known her as a "sinner", and in the story things got interesting when both the "good" (respected) and the "bad" (despised) ended up in the same house serving Jesus at the same time—one invited him to dine at his house, the other wiped his feet.

These two individuals could not be more different. They had totally different social and religious statuses, backgrounds, and reputations. Now they were serving Jesus in very different ways; indeed, with very different mindsets and motivations as well.

We often encourage brothers and sisters in the church to serve God and the community. This story provides us with a great opportunity to learn and reflect on what it really means to serve the Lord. The point of the story here is not to examine what went wrong with each of the two individuals' service to Jesus. Here the focus is not on comparing who serves God better, but rather addressing the issue of our worthiness in serving the Lord. Who is qualified to serve God?

Simon the Pharisee believed that the woman wasn't worthy or qualified to serve Jesus because she was a sinner. He thought in his heart, "If Jesus were a prophet, how could he allow this sinner to touch and defile him?" (verse 39). What he was really thinking was that this woman was unqualified to serve Jesus, and surely not as qualified as he was. She was a sinner; how dare she serve the Lord or even touch him? Shouldn't Jesus be smart enough to be aware of that too?

Jesus knew everything in Simon's heart, and he responded to the self-righteous thoughts in his heart by telling a story and raising a question that seemed unrelated:

In Luke 7:41-43, Jesus said:

> **41** Two people owed money to a certain moneylender. One owed him five hundred denarii, and the other fifty. **42** Neither of them had the money to pay him back, so he forgave the debts of both. Now which of them will love him more?"

> **43** Simon replied, "I suppose the one who had the bigger debt forgiven."

"You have judged correctly," Jesus said.

Jesus seemed to be affirming Simon for giving the correct answer. Was Jesus saying, "Right you are, Simon"?

Jesus' response revealed that he knew exactly what Simon was thinking, as well as who the woman was. But at first glance, Jesus' answer seemed a bit off-topic. The original question was about who was more worthy or qualified to serve Jesus. So why did Jesus suddenly bring in a story about debt? What's the relationship between debt and sin?

Indebtedness and sin are indeed very closely related, and the Bible links these two together several times. Every person has sinned and defied God. Therefore, we all owe God a debt. One of the lines in the Lord's Prayer, "Forgive us our debts", equates sins that need to be forgiven with debts. The problem of humanity is that the debt we owe God is a one that no one is ever able to repay.

One of the men in the parable owed the moneylender 500 hundred taels of silver, while the other owed fifty. Their debts were obviously different in magnitude, but they were both unable to repay them, and the creditor graciously forgave both of them. We are all exactly like the debtors when we sin against God. None of us can ever repay the debt we owe God. We are completely helpless and hopeless. Our only hope lies in our creditor's decision to give mercy and cancel the debt for us once and for all.

In Jesus' time, fifty taels of silver were equivalent to five hundred coins. A day's salary would be around one coin. This means that one man owed his creditor 500 days' wages, while the other owed fifty days'. In ancient times, there was no social welfare system. A worker would have to work without food for fifty days to pay off his debts. In other words, both debtors were unable to pay their debt, despite the difference in the amount.

When we say we are "Christians," what we are saying is that we are indebted to God, but Jesus has paid all our debts. The fact that we no longer need to repay our debts is only because of what Jesus did on the cross. We sinners are meant to be sentenced to death, but Jesus died in our place, and we therefore no longer need to face the sentence. This is why sin and the forgiveness of debt are closely connected in the Scriptures.

To understand God's grace, we must first see the stark reality that our debt to God can never be repaid. We probably know this in our heads, but not always in our hearts. Jesus' response to the self-righteous Simon pointed out that Simon himself also owed God what he could not pay. When we talk about serving God, we first need to return to the starting point of gratitude. Why should we serve God? The only reason is that we are all saved by grace. We have absolutely no room for feeling superior to other debtors. Simon mistakenly thought that he was more qualified to serve the Lord than the woman was.

The longer we have been Christians, or the more we serve God, the easier it is for us to forget we are just debtors who have been forgiven. Over time, we gradually start to have this subtle prideful thought that we are better or more worthy than people who are "not as good" a Christian as we are. There's a sense of superiority when we serve people whom we think have sinned more than we have. However, we must always remember that we are also hopeless debtors saved by God's mercy alone.

I have a few Christian friends who serve in prison ministries. They have shared amazing stories with me about what they have learned from the inmates they minister to. One thing that came across strongly to them when they came into contact with prisoners on death row or life without parole was these prisoners' total humility. These inmates are constantly aware of the fact that their debts of sin can never be repaid—something we Christians are not always conscious of. Their hopelessness highlights the vastness of God's mercy, and when they found forgiveness in God, their sense of freedom and gratitude was beyond measure.

Being forgiven is the greatest gift you can ever have if you know the magnitude of your debt. The point of this story is not that we should commit greater sins to love God more or to experience this joy of forgiveness more. The point is we must know how much indebted we are. We serve God out of pure gratitude and love, not out of a self-qualified, self-righteous, and self-justifying attitude.

If we ask questions like, "Are we qualified to serve God? Who's more qualified to serve God?" we're simply asking the wrong questions. Let's get back to Jesus' question: "Who loves Jesus more?". The answer is the one who owes more debt, because she knows the love of God is great.

Next, we see how Jesus applied this story in verses 44-47. What does this response of love look like?

> 44 Then he turned toward the woman and said to Simon, "Do you see this woman? I came into your house. You did not give me any water for my feet, but she wet my feet with her tears and wiped them

with her hair. **45** You did not give me a kiss, but this woman, from the time I entered, has not stopped kissing my feet. **46** You did not put oil on my head, but she has poured perfume on my feet. **47** Therefore, I tell you, her many sins have been forgiven—as her great love has shown. But whoever has been forgiven little loves little." (Luke 7:44-47)

How did Simon and the woman differ in the way they served Jesus? Jesus pointed out that when he entered the house, Simon did not wash his feet, kiss him, or anoint his head with oil. Why would he? He's the worthy host, the "good" God-fearing man. These duties were done by servants or slaves. Simon believed that he had done his part well as a host by inviting Jesus to come to his home and having the servants prepare the meal. In the context of Jesus' parable, Simon simply could not see he was actually a hopeless debtor at the mercy of the creditor.

What did the woman do for Jesus? Frankly speaking, she hardly did anything 'practical' for Jesus. She simply brought a bottle of perfume, went to see Jesus and started crying as soon as she was with him. She couldn't help the tears from her eyes wetting Jesus' feet, which was a socially embarrassing scene for her. She dried his feet with her hair, kissed them, and poured perfume on them in front of a group of judging men. Were these actions originally planned by the woman? Probably not. She simply couldn't hold back her tears. Jesus made it clear that the reason for her actions was because she loved the Lord so much. She was naturally moved by her gratitude inside her.

In other words, this woman understood her debt to Jesus. She was the forgiven one and was full of gratitude to Jesus, to the point of weeping uncontrollably. She saw Jesus as her saviour and her only hope. Simon the Pharisee, on the other hand, saw Jesus as a "guest". He even questioned the intelligence of his guest in his heart! He was wondering if this guest was good enough, not knowing that he himself was the one who wasn't good enough. His inner thoughts revealed he had no idea what the Gospel was really about. When Jesus asked, "Which one loves him more?", the answer was, of course, the woman who saw the richness of God's grace and unconditional love.

Is Jesus your saviour, or just your "guest"?

Jesus continued to say, "Therefore, I tell you, her many sins have been forgiven—as her great love has shown. But whoever has been forgiven little loves little." (verse 47).

Please do not misunderstand this verse. When Jesus was saying, "because of her love," the word "because" indicates that this is where the evidence lies. Jesus was not saying, "I forgive your sin because you have loved me more or because you served me well." Instead, Jesus was saying that her sins had *already* been forgiven. Her beautiful service to Jesus was her response to that forgiveness and a sign of her salvation, not the cause.

When we serve God out of our love and gratitude for God's grace, it is a sign that we have already been forgiven. If you think your acts of service are for repaying your debt, you will never succeed no matter how hard you try. The Scripture tells us we cannot, will not, and need not repay our debts. In Jesus, we are already forgiven. This is the Gospel.

What are your motivations for serving God? What exactly do you serve Him for? Is it out of a great sense of love for God, or just to fulfil a duty? Is it based on a desire to gain God's acceptance with your own effort, or an attempt to repay an impossible debt? Is it because it makes you feel good about yourself or feel like you are worthy enough to do it? How often do we reflect on our real, hidden intentions?

God does not require us to repay any of our debts to Him. He has already paid them in full with the blood of His own Son. This radical truth is not only for us to know in our heads, but also to experience it with all our heart and soul and be transformed by it every day. May we come before God's throne and serve Him with a heart that fully reflects the radical message of the cross.

12.

Haven't you got any fish?

(John 21:1-14)

Jesus had conquered death and risen from the dead! But after his resurrection, many of his most loyal disciples and closest friends were yet to be convinced. Jesus appeared to many people and asked many strange but profound questions. He asked Mary, "Why are you crying?". He asked Peter, "Do you love me more than these?". And he asked doubting Thomas, "Have you believed because you have seen me?".

These were all fundamental questions for the disciples to ponder as they encountered the risen Messiah, one who was so different from what they had expected. However, one question Jesus asked his disciples by the beach seemed the strangest of all: "Haven't you any fish?" (John 21:5).

Anyone who has read through the four Gospels knows very well that Jesus loved eating with his disciples, friends, and anyone who welcomed him. This was not the first time Jesus had asked people if they had anything to eat or drink. In feeding the five thousand, Jesus also asked his disciples what food they had (John 6), and in the story of the woman at the well, Jesus asked the Samaritan woman for a drink (John 4).

In both encounters, we know Jesus obviously wasn't really asking for food or drink for himself. He surely wasn't asking in order to enquire what was on the menu. On the contrary, Jesus wanted them to look, reflect, and ask him questions! He wanted them to be aware of the limits of what they had, to realize that they themselves didn't have enough, and to experience first-hand the abundance of provision available in Jesus. He wanted them to ask him for food and drink.

Now let's take a look at John 21:1-14:

> **1** Afterward Jesus appeared again to his disciples, by the Sea of Galilee. It happened this way: **2** Simon Peter, Thomas (also known as Didymus), Nathanael from Cana in Galilee, the sons of Zebedee, and two other disciples were together. **3** "I'm going out to fish," Simon Peter told them, and they said, "We'll go with you." So they went out and got into the boat, but that night they caught nothing. **4** Early in the morning, Jesus stood on the shore, but the disciples did not realize that it was Jesus. **5** He called out to them, "Friends, haven't you any fish?" "No," they answered. **6** He said, "Throw your net on the right side of the boat and you will find some." When they did, they were unable to haul the net in because of the large number of fish. **7** Then the disciple whom Jesus loved said to Peter, "It is the Lord!" As soon as Simon Peter heard him say, "It is the Lord," he wrapped his outer garment around him (for he had taken it off) and jumped into the water. **8** The other disciples followed in the boat, towing the net

full of fish, for they were not far from shore, about a hundred yards. **9** When they landed, they saw a fire of burning coals there with fish on it, and some bread. **10** Jesus said to them, "Bring some of the fish you have just caught." **11** So Simon Peter climbed back into the boat and dragged the net ashore. It was full of large fish, 153, but even with so many the net was not torn. **12** Jesus said to them, "Come and have breakfast." None of the disciples dared ask him, "Who are you?" They knew it was the Lord. **13** Jesus came, took the bread and gave it to them, and did the same with the fish. **14** This was now the third time Jesus appeared to his disciples after he was raised from the dead.

Jesus appeared to his beloved disciples by greeting them with a question (John 21:5), "Haven't you any fish?"

Was it just a friendly greeting, like when we meet a friend on a fishing trip? Jesus clearly knew the disciples hadn't caught any fish and were struggling to do so. So Jesus' question was, in a sense, a rhetorical one. Jesus wasn't saying, "Hi guys! How's fishing going this morning?". Nor was he saying, "Hey! What fish have you got? Let me try some!"

The NASB translation captures the tone of the question very well, which a classical Greek reader may have also picked up: "You do not have any fish, do you?". In other words, Jesus was asking an embarrassing question to remind the disciples, "You are aware you aren't getting what you need, right?".

Why was Jesus asking that question?

Let's return to the story. Note that the question Jesus was asking was quite ironic. The scene we have here is not an experienced fisherman trying to help someone who does not know how to fish. Jesus, a carpenter and rabbi, was challenging a group of professional fishermen. Fishing was what they knew best all their lives. Catching fish was what they did for a living. It was their identity. These fishermen had everything: equipment, expertise, manpower, and a lake full of fish. But Jesus' question instantly exposed their limitations and inability.

Throughout the Bible, God often wants us to recognize and experience our own limitations when we try to accomplish things by ourselves. Most of us are not fishermen, but we are "in the same boat" as Peter and other fishermen in the story. We like to think we have what we need, even in our walk with God. We want to bear fruit. We want to be the person God has created us to be. We want to glorify God. We want to grow in maturity. But we struggle, we doubt, and we fail. Jesus is asking, "You do not have what you need, do you?".

This is exactly what Jesus was teaching when he taught us the Lord's Prayer. We are to ask God for His daily provision because we're insufficient in ourselves. We ask for forgiveness as we forgive others. We ask God to deliver us from evil. We can't do any of these things by ourselves. The Lord's Prayer isn't just about asking God to provide for our needs, but also about bringing us to a true realization of our needs.

Jesus' analogy of the vine and branches (John 15) also points to this exact lesson. We, as branches, can never bear any fruit unless we remain in Jesus, the vine. Without being connected to the vine, the branches simply become totally useless. But when connected, they can bear fruit in abundance.

We need, first, to recognize our insufficiency. Here in the story, the disciples had yet to even recognize Jesus! So how would they recognize him?

When you read different stories of Jesus appearing to his disciples after his resurrection in the four Gospels, you'll notice that in almost all the incidents the disciples couldn't recognize Jesus at first. Think about the story of the two disciples on the road to Emmaus. The people had a long conversation with Jesus without knowing they were actually speaking to Jesus himself. Mary, weeping in anguish on the most joyful day of history, was not even aware that she was in fact talking directly with Jesus.

But do you notice any pattern in how people began to recognize Jesus? Every time, once Jesus started doing something he had done with them previously, they immediately recognized him. For instance, when Jesus broke bread, the disciples on the road to Emmaus had their eyes opened (Luke 24:31). Likewise, when Jesus called Mary by her name at the tomb, she recognized the Lord and shouted with joy (John 20:16).

This time, Jesus told them, "Throw your net on the right side of the boat, and you will find some fish" (John 21: 6). The Scripture tells us that "when they did, they were unable to haul the net in because of the large number of fish" (21:7). Of course, if you still can't recognize Jesus at the sight of the miraculous catch of fish, you're pretty slow. Jesus had not only performed this familiar act of catching fish with them before (Luke 5), but he was also surely the only one who was able to catch fish miraculously like that.

We often feel God is asking us to do all sorts of impossible things. Love our enemies? Carry our cross and follow Jesus? Love God with all our heart, soul, strength, and mind? Forgive people seventy-seven times? Take the Gospel to all ends of the earth? These are all impossible things. The more we try, the more we feel defeated.

When Jesus told Peter he would be a "fisher of men" (this command is recorded in all four Gospels), for Peter, Jesus was calling him to do something impossible. Sometimes he could hardly catch fish like a proper fisherman!

But every difficult command from God is also a promise from God. Have you ever thought about this? God isn't giving harsh instruction to make us feel inadequate, to trick us into failing, or to make us work extra hard. With every command, God is making a promise: He will enable us to do it. All things are possible in him and only in Him. He invites us to experience the impossible in Him. Yes, you can love your enemies. Yes, you can carry the Gospel to the ends of the earth. In Jesus, you can.

In the story, these fishermen were letting go of their pride, understanding, reputation, and professionalism, and putting their trust in Jesus. But their work wasn't finished. In verse 8, after they had caught the fish, they still needed to bring the fish up to the boat, then to the shore. The bigger the catch, the more difficult the task.

While they were doing so, Jesus was already getting ready to enjoy breakfast with them. Jesus could have multiplied the bread and fish, like in the miracle he had performed when feeding the five thousand, but this time he empowered his disciples to catch the fish and experience the abundance of 'fruit' when they remained in him.

In narrating the story, John chose to record the exact number of fish caught: a total of 153. That is a heavy load! What is the significance of the number 153? Many scholars have tried to "decode" this number by searching for clues in the Old Testament. However, the Bible is not a book of hidden clues and riddles. Very often, the simplest explanation is the best explanation. John simply wanted to tell the readers they had managed to count the fish, which implied the net had not torn this time! It would be impossible to count them if the net was broken. Remember, last time that was what had happened (Luke 5:6). God's supply is abundant, His provision is sufficient, and His way always sustains.

Like the disciples, we all look forward to a day when we can enjoy a feast with Jesus. The Bible tells us this feast is not a reward for our hard work or capabilities. Instead, it requires us to first recognize our own inadequacies and insufficiencies in fulfilling what is required of us. Only then can we experience the abundance in Jesus and God's power in making the impossible transformation possible. This is how we know the Gospel is real and so much more precious than anything we know in life.

What change do you want to see in your life that you believe is impossible? What change do you think God wants to see in your life? Do we recognize Jesus being there with us? If Jesus asked you today, "Haven't you got any _______?", what would be in the blank for you? Turn to Jesus and ask him for what you need. He is more than willing to give it to you.

Reflection questions

As this book is aimed to facilitate both personal devotions and group interactions, here are some questions you may reflect on while engaging with each chapter:

1. Which part of the story strikes you most?
2. Would Jesus be asking you this same question he asked in the story? If yes, what do you think he is trying to say and why?
3. How would you answer him? What may be hindering you?
4. How may your life and perspectives be different after this encounter with Jesus?
5. Who can you share this story with?

Acknowledgements

This translation project is possible because of the diligent help of various brothers and sisters of Emmanuel Chinese Church (Hong Kong) who have recorded, archived, transcribed, and generously shared their church's sermon resources freely with the public over many years.

A group of my parents' old friends from their university days, known as 'CA74' (which stands for Christian Association, class of '74), have not only funded the expenses of this publication, but also provided much prayer support and encouragement throughout the process. My family is greatly indebted to them.

We would like to express our heartfelt thanks to Dr. Sven Soderlund, my father's Advisor as well as biblical Hebrew and Greek teacher when he was at Regent College, Canada (1978-80), for kindly writing the Foreword for this publication. Dr. Soderlund's caring and supportive approach to his advisees was fondly and gratefully remembered, and my parents treasured their friendship with him.

Did you love *Jesus' Awkward Questions*? Then you should read *True Calling, False Calling: How the Bible Draws the Line* by Philip Yeung!

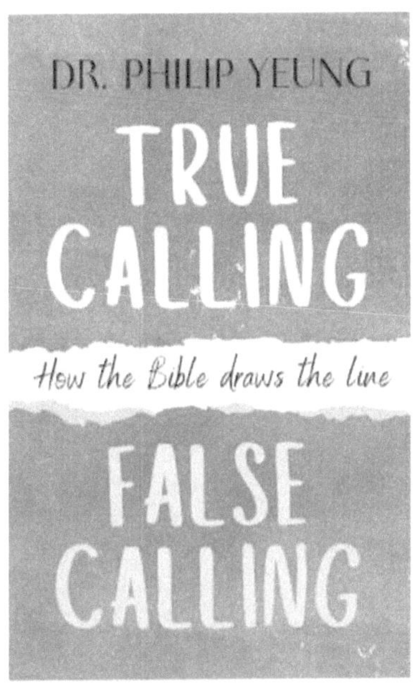

In discerning God's calling, many Christians find themselves looking for elusive 'signs', attending special conferences, or doing some spiritual aptitude tests. Yet in the Bible, God has never asked anyone to do these things. In fact, the Biblical approach to understanding one's calling is surprisingly straightforward, yet profound. This book isn't your average guide to 'find your potential' or 'discover God's plan.' By debunking popular myths about God's calling, Dr. Philip Yeung delivers a truthful exploration of the essence of God's calling as manifested in 24 Bible stories. (Coming Dec 2023)

Also by Philip Yeung

Jesus' Awkward Questions
Darkest Night, Brightest Dawn: A Lent Reflection

About the Author

Rev. Dr. Philip Yeung (Yeung Sek Cheung) was raised in Hong Kong and trained as a medical doctor at the University of Hong Kong. Five years into his practice, he believed God called him to leave his profession to serve in theological education in Hong Kong. After graduating from Regent College, Canada, he devoted the next 40 years of his life to teaching at China Graduate School of Theology, where he specialized in the teaching of biblical languages, the books of Genesis, Job and Ecclesiastes, as well as homiletics and pastoral care. His medical training, his proficiency in both Biblical Hebrew and Greek, and his journey in discovering God's calling, all equipped him with insights into stories in the Bible as well as the ability to dissect them and help his students apply them in modern life.